Lighting the Path of
Righteousness

Jerry Stafford

PAGE PUBLISHING, INC.
New York, NY

First originally published by Page Publishing, Inc. 2018

ISBN 978-1-64214-528-1 (Paperback)
ISBN 978-1-64214-529-8 (Digital)

Printed in the United States of America

CONTENTS

"Nobody really knows for sure if they're going to heaven or not. If you ask them, they will tell you they know, but they really don't."

I sat quietly in my seat, but inside, I was seething with frustration. I was very disturbed that a pastor of long experience and a retired air force chaplain who claimed to endorse the doctrine of his denomination could make a statement like that.

It should have been no surprise. I had struggled with that very question for several years and had just completed a study of 1 John. I turned to that little book in the Bible now to make sure of the answers.

Is that pastor correct? A study of 1 John should be more than enough to convince anyone of the truth as the light on the path of righteousness reveals the truth.

CHAPTER 1

A Christian Testimony Provides Light That Can Lead to the Path of Righteousness

1 John 1:1–4

A Christian testimony is the result of a personal encounter with Jesus. When we were children in the Oklahoma hills, one of our pastimes was to pick the petals from a sunflower bloom or a daisy, while saying with each petal, "She loves me, she loves me not." Thankfully, we don't have to do those kinds of things to determine whether God loves us or not because there is a way of knowing. That is through the knowledge gained by experiencing a personal relationship with Jesus Christ, his Son.

How can we know? How can we confirm our experience in Christ? There are some ways we can know; hopefully, some of these can be revealed in this attempt to describe my own Christian experience.

I was the fifth child born to a family of thirteen in 1934, during the depression. We lived in the back country of Oklahoma in houses that were usually too small or too ran down for most people to live in. Most of the time, we were barebacked, barefooted, and bareheaded. We did each have a pair of shoes to wear to town and to school and clothes mostly given to us by neighbors and others. When someone came to visit, we would normally hide until they left.

Our mother claimed to be a Jehovah's Witness but did not participate in their activities. My father did not profess to believe anything concerning Christianity and, for the most part, lived a very honest but rough life.

A personal encounter with Jesus can be initiated by a faithful witness.

One day, a lady who lived down the road from us drove into the yard in a pickup with a homemade camper shell on the back of it. We soon learned her name was Violet Hobbs, and she wanted us to ride to Elm Grove Pentecostal Church with her the next Sunday morning.

A personal encounter with Jesus provides spiritual light that leads to the path of righteousness.

I believe God sent Violet Hobbs there that day to call me to Christ because while going to that church, I was saved. I didn't know about formal things like baptism and church membership because nobody bothered to tell me, but one thing I knew and know is my life was changed by that experience forever.

I was introduced to Jesus, and he became an integral part of my life. Salvation is a change of heart, a change of mind, and a change of behavior. I can testify to that change.

We moved away and I moved on, but I continued to pray and search for information about God, but because my background was one of complete ignorance concerning the church and the Bible, I continued to wander from one point to another in my search for the truth with that and a confused hunger for spiritual fulfillment.

At the age of fourteen, I ran away from home and went to live with one of my many uncles. He was Sunday school superintendent in a church in Lawton, Oklahoma. Almost every Sunday for the year I was there, I went forward "to receive the gift of tongues" because they believed you could only be saved that way.

I went forward in several Baptist churches as time went on to "make a profession of faith." I filled out their cards and said their little prayers but that was as far as it went. Nobody reached out to explain the need for baptism or church membership or the many other things I needed to know to grow in my faith and understanding. After all,

I was very poor and "wild as a March hare." Consequently, it seemed to me nobody was interested in me.

I was drafted into the army at the age of twenty-one. By that time, I was married and had a baby daughter. I was a very reluctant servant, but the Lord knew what he was doing. I went through basic training at Fort Carson, Colorado. When I had finished basic training, I was sent to Fort Rucker, Alabama, to become an aircraft mechanic.

We didn't even know where Fort Rucker, Alabama, was so we bought a ticket to Birmingham. We found a taxi and asked the driver to take us to Fort Rucker. With a little laugh, he informed us there was no Fort Rucker around there and took us back to the bus station where we were informed that Fort Rucker was near a town called Enterprise.

We bought tickets and arrived in Enterprise that afternoon confused and bewildered but determined to see what we could figure out.

Someone told us of a motel on the west edge of town. We caught a ride to the motel. I can't remember if it was a taxi or somebody in their personal car.

While we were in the process of renting the room, the lady who owned and operated the small motel asked us about our situation. I explained that we were supposed to be stationed at Fort Rucker, and we would need a place to stay.

"I know someone," she said. "My brother-in-law has a place about five miles from base. The next day, we rented his little house. It was great because it was only about a quarter of a mile from a little grocery store.

We walked up to the little store the next morning. While we were shopping, the lady behind the counter asked us about church. I confessed that we had not been in a long time. "There's one just down the road south," she said. "Sunday school starts at nine forty-five and preaching is at eleven."

We accepted that invitation and soon were accepted as members by profession of our faith and were baptized in what was then known as Daleville Baptist Church but is now known as Mount

Liberty Baptist Church. Soon after our baptism, I received orders for Hawaii. My wife, Betty, with our daughter, Teresa, went to live with her parents until preparations could be made for them to join me.

While in Hawaii, we attended a Christian church. Soon after we started going there, we were accepted into the church as a part of their Watch Care Program. It was an opportunity for us to learn more about God and experience spiritual growth.

When our time of service in Hawaii was finished, we were sent to Fort Ord, California. Soon after our arrival there, we joined and became quite involved with the activities at First Baptist Church in Marina.

Several months after joining that church, I surrendered to the ministry and have seen the Lord perform miracles in many lives since that time.

I strongly believe God sent Violet Hobbs to the home of a shy, ignorant country boy in a remote rural area of Oklahoma over fifty years ago so that I might know him. I believe God arranged for me to be drafted into the army to become an aircraft mechanic. You see, when they made me an aircraft mechanic, I had never seen an aircraft on the ground, but had I not become an aircraft mechanic, I would not have gone to Fort Rucker, Alabama, nor would I have been baptized upon my profession of Jesus as my Lord and Savior at Mount Liberty Baptist Church, where I later preached my first sermon, nor would have a lot of other things happened to me for his glory.

I apologize for brevity. We have seen God open and build churches, rescue individuals from the brink of death, and change lives, but space doesn't permit me to tell the whole story.

Spiritual Light Reveals the Identity of Christ

He is revealed as God in the flesh. Perhaps you have seen the commercial on TV where Santa meets the M&Ms and says, "They are real," and one of the M&Ms says, "He is real!" and they all fall to the floor. That kind of reaction to recognition of the reality of Jesus's existence is not imperative for a Christian experience. However,

Hebrews 11:6 does tell us: "Without faith it is impossible to please God, because anyone who comes to him must believe that he exists and that he rewards those who earnestly seek him."

Spiritual Light Creates a Personal Encounter with Jesus

John offers this testimony: "That which we have heard, which we have seen with our eyes, which we have looked upon and our hands have handled" (1 John 1:1b).

Although none of us today can testify to a physical experience such as the one described by the writer of 1 John, we can attest to a personal experience confirmed through accepting that testimony as true and relevant to his presence. In the Preacher's Homiletic Commentary, this assertion is made: "Let any man now come into close personal relations with Christ, let him feel the impression which Christ always makes, when he is permitted to come fully into the sphere of a man's thought, and heart and life, and he will surely be drawn to the "Man Christ Jesus," and will bow before him, saying, "My Lord and my God." (1)

We are informed by Paul in Romans 8:16 that: "The Spirit himself testifies with our spirit that we are God's children." Many have struggled with this verse; looking for a preconceived emotional experience of anointing like that of the apostle Paul, while he was known as Saul, or some other similar example like the one in Acts 9:1–9. There are, however, about as many variations in response as there are conversions. In Acts 8:26–39, the story is told of the conversion of the Ethiopian Eunuch. The picture presented here is one of an individual who simply believed, was baptized and rejoiced because of his conversion.

The experience of the Philippian Jailer can be described as similar to that of the Ethiopian Eunuch: "The Jailer then called for lights, rushed in and fell trembling before Paul and Silas. He then brought them out and asked, 'Sirs, what must I do to be saved?' They replied, 'Believe in the Lord Jesus Christ, and you will be saved—you and your household.' Then they spoke the word of the Lord to him and to all others in the house. At that hour of the night the jailer took them and washed their wounds, then immediately he and all his family were baptized." (2)

Spiritual Light Reveals Christ as One Who Has An Everlasting Existence

Twice in Revelation the term is used to describe him as "The Alpha and the Omega" (Revelations 1:8 and 22:13). In the Gospel of John, he claims his everlasting existence. In John 8:58 he says, "Most assuredly, I say unto you, before Abraham was I am"

He Was the Beginning of All Things

Guy H. King quoted Dr. Marvin Vincent who says, "*In* implies being present before the creation and *from* signifies presence at the time of creation," (3) either word establishes the everlastingness of Jesus.

In 1 John 1:1, it points him out as, "That which was from the beginning."

John 1:1–3 makes an even more emphatic statement when that writer says, "In the beginning was the Word (Christ) and the word was with God and the Word was God. He was with God in the beginning. Through Him all things were made; without Him nothing was made that was made."

It has always amused me that so much time and money are spent in search for the beginning and "evolution" of things when the answer is so simple and apparent. The Bible explains the whole thing in one short sentence: "In the beginning, God created the heavens and the earth" (Genesis 1:1).

There is a simple explanation for the confusion of science and the confidence of Christianity. The difference can be described by one word: *faith*. Hebrews 11:1 offers this description of faith: "Now faith is being sure of what we hope for and certain of what we do not see."

In the first part of Hebrews 11:6, the Bible says, "Without faith it is impossible to please God." Hebrews 11:3 points out the power, and the preciousness of faith with these words, "By faith we understand that the universe was formed at God's command, so that what is seen was not made out of what was visible."

As research progresses, more evidence is revealed that favors creation and disputes the theories of many scientists whose interest is served by removing God from world history.

He Is the End of All Things

We are reminded by Paul in 1 Corinthians 15:19 that our hope for joy and fulfillment is not in this life. There we are informed that "If only for this life we have hope in Christ, we are to be pitied more than all men."

Most of the fifteenth chapter of First Corinthians deals with the resurrection, there is an argument over whether Christ was indeed resurrected, then an argument as to whether we would be resurrected in a spiritual body or a different kind of body. Today there are discussions about when the rapture (the taking up of Christians into heaven) will happen and in what way.

In all the discussions and speculation there are a few things we must remember that Jesus has promised to come for us in the fullness of time. That God has promised to put all our enemies under his feet, including death and that he has prepared a place for us to spend eternity.

It is up to him to name the time and the method in which he will come for us but it will happen. He told his disciples in John 14:2–3: "In my Father's house, there are many rooms (spaces); if it were not true, I would have told you. I am going there to prepare a place for you, and if I go and prepare a place for you, I will come back and take you to be with me that you may also be where I am." (4)

That should be sufficient for an individual who has placed his or her faith in God.

He is imminently present today. That presence is more than an internal witness or strong faith. It is a revealed experience. I personally have seen God intervene in life situations beyond human capability. One of those events happened while I was stationed in Germany.

It was noon, and I had come home for lunch. The phone rang and my wife answered it. It was one of the ladies from Hahn Baptist Church, Germany, where I was pastor at the time. She spoke in a very excited voice, and I expected the worst. I was almost right.

"Pastor," she said, "there's been an accident. Tom and Ellie's son, Mike, (not their real names) fell out of one of the apartment windows and landed on his head on a coal chute. They have him in an ambulance right now, and they are taking him to Wiesbaden Hospital." Wiesbaden Air Force Base Hospital was about seventy miles from where they lived at Hahn Air Force Base and fifty from my home in Baumholder.

After praying with her over the phone, I instructed her to gather all the people she could find and start the prayer chain. "I'll call Brother Wilbur and have his church do the same," I informed her. After asking my wife and daughters to pray, I called my supervisor and told him I wouldn't be back from lunch, changed my clothes, and jumped in my old beat-up Chevy station wagon and headed to Wiesbaden Air Force Base Hospital, praying as I drove.

When I arrived, Ellie informed me that little Mike was critical, in a coma, and hovering on the edge of life. We went to his bedside and held hands and prayed for him.

We continued praying for him for about two weeks. Other churches came and visited Ellie and Tom and prayed, but there was no apparent change until one day a pastor from a neighboring church, the deacons from that church, Tom and I went to the chapel to pray.

After each of us had prayed, except Tom—he was not a Christian at that time—and prepared to leave, Tom said, "Stay and talk with me. I want to be a Christian." We stayed and I counseled with him, and he surrendered his life to Christ.

We returned to the waiting room and visited for a short time before I left to go home. I can't remember if it was that day or the next when Ellie called to say, "He's better!"

In less than two weeks, that baby was ready to come home. I believe God answered our prayers. (5)

I can attest to the fact that God answers prayer. He has answered mine and the answers to Tom's prayer, and mine is proof to me of the presence of God in the world today: "Dear friends, if our hearts do not condemn us, we have confidence before God and receive anything we ask, because we obey his commands and do what pleases him" (1 John 3:21–22).

Christians recognize Christ as Savior. The last part of 1 John 1:1 puts it like this: "This we proclaim concerning the Word of Life." In 1 John 4:14, the reason for Jesus having come in the flesh is confirmed and makes it completely clear when he says, "And we have seen and testify that the Father has sent the Son to be the Savior of the world."

It cannot be emphasized too often or too much that the writer of 1 John had walked with Jesus during his earthly ministry, had eaten meals with him, had witnessed his crucifixion, had witnessed his resurrection along with more than five hundred others, and had personally witnessed his ascension and heard the promise of his return. All that time, he had heard Jesus testify of his mission to "seek and save that which is lost."

He had seen miracle after miracle. He had witnessed Jesus's love and compassion. Those experiences made an indelible impression on his life and we have the privilege of being made aware of his personal experience with God in the flesh, the Savior of the world.

Because I accept and believe the story of John's personal experience with Jesus, I am one of many who are convinced of his authority on the subject and that recognition of Jesus as Lord brings us to the realization that he is also Savior. He must be Lord to be our Savior.

Christians Recognize Christ as Lord

"Therefore, God exalted him to the highest place and gave him the name that is above every name that at the name of Jesus every knee should bow in heaven and on earth and every tongue confess that Jesus Christ is Lord to the glory of God the Father." (6)

It is not unusual for people to address Jesus as Lord but I wonder how many grasp the significance of that title. There are at least three reasons Jesus is Lord.

The first reason for calling Jesus *Lord* is that he is our creator. If you make something, you expect to have some control over it. With that in mind, consider the definition of the word *lord* as defined in Unger's Bible Dictionary as, "An early word denoting ownership; hence absolute control." (7)

(The Holman Illustrated Bible Dictionary defines the word *lord* as, "An English rendering of several Hebrew and Greek words. Generally, the term refers to one who has power and authority.") (8)

Jesus informed the disciples of his Lordship by saying, "All authority has been given to me in heaven and on earth" (Matthew 28:18). (The King James Version of the Bible uses the word power here instead of authority.) This truth was demonstrated repeatedly during the time he spent living among us as he went about healing those who suffered from sickness and disease, casting out demons, and demonstrating his great power in many ways.

Jesus is Lord because he redeemed us. The apostle Paul tells the church at Corinth, "You are not your own; you were bought with a price, therefore glorify God with your body" (1 Corinthians 6:20). When Adam and Eve chose to eat of the forbidden fruit in the Garden of Eden, they sold their souls into slavery to Satan. Because they are the federal head of all mankind, we inherited that bondage, consequently a ransom had to be paid for our freedom from Satan and the consequences of sin.

Paul addresses that dilemma when he informs us that the wages (price) for sin is death, but the gift of God is eternal life through Jesus Christ our Lord (Romans 6:23). In his letter to Timothy, he points out that Jesus gave himself "as a ransom for all men" (1 Timothy 2:6).

Jesus, as Lord, eventually will be our Judge. Wow! What a transition. The same Jesus who came into the world to be our Savior will be Lord and judge, and one day we will all stand before him to account for ourselves.

The apostle Paul informs us, "It is written, 'As surely as I live,' says the Lord, every knee will bow before me; every tongue will confess to God. So then, each of us will give an account of himself to God."

This is an opportunity to become entangled with several different beliefs about eschatology (the end times). I hope to avoid that discussion because it is not part of this discussion. What is important here is whether Jesus is Lord of your life or not. If you have never accepted Jesus as Savior and made him Lord of your life, the day you stand before him, he will be your judge.

Spiritual Communication Lights the Path of Righteousness.

As John is giving a testimony of his experience, he is keenly aware that it is a testimony designed to attract others to salvation through a personal encounter with Jesus. "The life appeared; we have seen it and do testify of it, and we proclaim to you the eternal life which was with the Father and has appeared to us" (1 John 1:2).

Spiritual communication provides light that reveals a call from God. If we are going to believe in the sovereign grace of God, it must be said that God initiates the call to salvation. Throughout this attempt to describe the Christian experience, one thing is apparent: Because Jesus is Lord, it is he who takes the initiative; as we study the scriptures, he is found approaching individuals who are totally involved in other activities.

It was he who went searching for Adam and Eve in the garden: "Then the man and his wife heard the sound of the Lord God as he was walking in the garden in the cool of the day, and they hid from the Lord God among the trees of the garden. But the Lord God called to the man, 'Where are you?'" (9)

It was he who went looking for Abraham while he sat among moon worshippers: "The Lord God had said to Abram, "Leave your country, your people and your father's household and go to a land

I will show you" (Genesis12:1). There are several more incidents in which he called individuals to do his bidding.

He went looking for David while he was still a shepherd boy. He rescued his people out of their dilemma while they were helpless in Egypt.

One can witness the act of drawing with Moses at the burning bush. Moses was apparently wandering along in the desert with his sheep and saw, "a bush burning yet not consumed." Look at his first response: "So Moses thought, 'I will go over and see this strange sight—why does the bush not burn up.' When he walked over to it, God spoke to him out of the burning bush" When the Lord saw that he had gone over to look, God called to him from within the bush, Moses! Moses." (10)

Not only is there a long list of examples in the Old Testament. There are many examples that confirm his taking the initiative in the New Testament as well. Jesus sought each of his disciples personally. Matthew 4:19 records his calling of Peter and Andrew, "Come follow me and I will make you fishers of men." Then he delivered an invitation to the world: "Come to me, all you who are weary and burdened and I will give you rest" (Matthew 11:28). Then again: "If anyone is thirsty, let him come and drink" (John 7:37).

He came to Saul "as one out of season." In the book of Revelation, he gives a vivid invitation: "Here I am! I stand at the door and knock. If anyone hears my voice and opens the door, I will come in and eat with him and he with me" (Revelations 3:20).

The conversion of Saul and of Isaiah—not to mention the Ethiopian Eunuch in Acts 7:34 and of the seller of purple in Acts 16:14—establishes irrefutable evidence that God, because of his grace, takes the initiative in our salvation. Ephesians 2:8 informs us: "For it is by grace you have been saved, through faith—and this not of yourselves it is a gift from God." In verse nine, he makes it even more clear when he continues "not of works lest anyone should boast."

Isaiah makes a vivid and amazing record of his calling. He said, "I saw the Lord high and exalted" (Isaiah 6:1). He could have been a regular church member or a prophet with no special message.

He regularly attended services; he worked around the church and probably even did some type of ministry. We really don't know what he was doing when he received his calling, but it is stated by some and implied by others that he had already been called to the position of prophet when he received the vision recorded in Isaiah 6:1–9. That was when the Lord appeared to him in the temple. When he "saw the Lord high and exalted," Isaiah 6:1 describes his experience this way: "In the year that king Uzziah died, I saw the Lord seated on a throne, high and exalted, and the train of his robe filled the temple."

To sum it up in simple language, God had come looking for him. Isaiah continues the next seven verses describing his personal experience with the Lord. In verse eight, the Bible says he heard a voice: "Then I heard the voice of the Lord saying, 'Whom shall we send? And who will go for us? And I said, 'Here am I, send me.'"

That statement has always seemed so profound to me. One of the past presidents of the Southern Baptist Convention stated conversion perfectly when he said, "It's not how high a man jumps when he gets religion, but how he walks when he hits the ground that makes a difference." (11)

Isaiah truly had had an experience with the Lord and was ready to do his will.

Spiritual communication provides light that causes conviction of sin. As we sense this call from God to become righteous, we become acutely aware of our own unrighteousness. With that awareness, the revelation from God of his desire and ability to bring about salvation becomes a part of that same awareness.

Conviction of our sin and our lack of perfection is like comparing a marred and imperfect object with one that is perfect.

Perhaps Isaiah is an even better example. What many of us call conviction is very clearly a part of his experience. In Isaiah 6:5 he said, "Woe to me! I cried, I am ruined for I am a man of unclean lips, and I live among a people of unclean lips, and my eyes have seen the King, the Lord Almighty."

Spiritual Communication Provides Light
that Reveals Our Inadequacy

We lived quite a distance from anyone, and our old car was broken down. It seems to me daddy had removed a major part from it when we noticed clouds gathering in the northwest.

In a few minutes, the storm had arrived. I watched through a window as the violently churning black clouds came rolling across the corral. Suddenly, a whitish looking funnel cloud dropped out of the blackness about a hundred yards from the house.

As my father watched that funnel spiral downward and move in our direction, he yelled in desperation and helplessness, "My God, help!" God helped. The tornado picked up and moved away.

We learned the next day that a tornado had struck a neighbor's farm two miles south of us. We went over there to help. Devastation and havoc were many. Dead animals were strewn here and there, the fence had been rolled up or destroyed, and the house was completely demolished, but the family had found protection in their barn. Half of it was built in the side of a hill, and they had found shelter there.

It is my belief that God responded to my father's feelings of inadequacy and answered his call for help. When we were, God helped. (12)

We are equally helpless in the spiritual sense when it comes to our eternal salvation. On the other hand, however, there is a scenario where I can picture God picking us up in the vehicle of faith because we are too weak and helpless to save our self. Paul tells us in Romans 5:6, "You see, at just the right time, when we were powerless, Christ died for the ungodly." Isaiah said in Isaiah 6:5, "Woe to me for I am ruined." He was aware of his inadequacy and was devastated by it. Listen to him as he recognizes his position in the presence of God: "I am a man of unclean lips and I live among a people of unclean lips, and my eyes have seen the King, the Lord Almighty."

We were on a field exercise several years ago in the Mojave dessert. My pilot had taken off for another airstrip and there was nobody there but me. Suddenly I was surrounded by army tanks. Although it was just a practice exercise, I still remember that feeling of helplessness as I stood there alone in that small clearing with all those tanks surrounding me with their guns seemingly pointed straight at me. As helpless as I was, had that situation been real, so we are all helpless when it comes to our salvation. (13)

If you are trying to save yourself through clean living or acts of goodness, please allow me to tell you it won't work; you need to be rescued. But wait! The penalty has been paid! Rescue has already been made possible! In 2 Corinthians 5:21, "God made him (Jesus) who had no sin to be sin for us, so that in him we might become the righteousness of God."

Spiritual communication provides light that reveals the need for confession. When Isaiah realized his sinfulness and his inadequacy to correct it he immediately experienced a strong need for confession. Notice the words of derision, "'Woe is me,' I cried, 'for I am undone.'" This is a perfect example of a confession. The Holman Illustrated Bible Dictionary makes this statement about confession of sin.

Numerous OT passages stress the importance of the confession of sin within the experience of worship. Leviticus speaks of ritual acts involving such admission of sin (or guilt) offering (5:5–6:7) and the scapegoat that represents the removal of sin (16:20–22). Furthermore, confession can be the act of an individual on behalf of all the people (Nehemiah 1:6; Daniel 9:20) or the collective response of the worshiping congregation (Ezra 10:1; Nehemiah 9:2–3. Frequently, it is presented as the individual acknowledgement of sin by the penitent sinner. (14)

Can you see a mental picture of Isaiah as he saw the "Lord sitting on a throne high and lifted up and his train filled the temple" (Isaiah 6:1)?

It is no wonder he stated: "Then said I, 'Woe is me! For I am undone!'" (Isaiah 6:5). His confession perfectly fits the definition offered above in the Holman Illustrated Bible Dictionary. (15) The contrition brought about by his feelings of inadequacy are to be sensed in those words of dismay he uttered.

Spiritual Light Reveals the Need and the Possibility for Cleansing

When I was about five years old, I was running across my aunt's backyard, barefoot as usual, and stepped on a broken glass and cut my big toe almost all the way off. My mother and my aunt Eunice took me to the doctor several miles away.

After the doctor had sewed my toe back on, we arrived back home to find one of my cousins, who was about a year younger than I, had fallen through one of the holes in the outdoor toilet. My Aunt Vera had fished him out and given him a thorough scrubbing then put a pair of her panties on him. (16)

There is no comparison, however, in the extent of Aunt Vera's act of mercy and what Jesus does spiritually for us. She could only cleanse the outside; the Bible teaches us that salvation is a cleansing of our soul. 1 John 1:9 in the New King James Bible tells us, "If we confess our sin, He is faithful and just to forgive us our sins and to cleanse us from all unrighteousness." That is the mercy of God in action. Cleansing from sin is not anything we have done, it is what Jesus made possible on the cross two thousand years ago, and his action was executed by the mercy of spiritual communication that provides light and reveals our need for repentance. An excellent example of conviction that leads to repentance through faith can be found in Acts 2:37. On the day of the Pentecost, Peter preached a long and convincing message on the need for repentance and the people responded with deep and sincere feeling: "When the people heard this, they were cut to the heart and said to Peter and the other apostles, 'Brothers, what shall we do?'"

The word *repentance* is a word that some struggle with, but Peter makes the necessity of it quite clear when he informs them: "Repent and be baptized, every one of you, in the name of Jesus Christ for the forgiveness of your sins. And you will receive the gift of the Holy Spirit."

Repentance was not the beginning of their salvation, but it certainly was an integral part of it. This is the point that one must arrive at through having believed by faith. Awesome power exists in the faith that brings us to the point of repentance.

Those listening to Peter's message in acts two were the same people who were demanding the crucifixion of Christ only fifty-three days previously, and now they are looking to him for forgiveness and salvation; that sounds like turning about or as some would say, "Turning from sin and self to Jesus Christ and making him Lord of your life."

Repentance was brought about because they believed the information they had just received through faith; therefore, we can say, "Faith is awareness that God is communicating with us to draw us into his presence and cause us to repent unto salvation."

The light that reveals our conviction comes to us through faith. Faith motivates individuals to examine their own life in comparison with the power and perfection of God.

Conviction of Our Sin Is Recognition That God Is Pointing Out Our Need for Repentance through Faith

Spiritual communication offers a message of exoneration. It's not just a matter of being guilty and convicted of sin. It is a matter of being convicted and convinced of exoneration. That is, recognizing Jesus as Savior. The conviction of Isaiah came when he saw the Lord "high and lifted up" (Isaiah 6:1). The conviction of the apostle Paul came when he was knocked off his high horse on the road to Damascus. These two men lived many years apart, but they were both convicted by the same God of their sins. They were both struck with the same awesome fear, and they both came to the same conclusion about their situation. What did they have in common? The same God who convicted them convinced them of the answer to their dilemma. Isaiah said, "I have seen the King of Glory."

The apostle Paul asked the very pertinent question, "Who are you Lord?" and received the answer, "I am Jesus, whom you are persecuting."

In each case, it was God who initiated the encounter and offered the solution. Because of his grace, he reached out to them. My Bible tells me in 2 Peter 3:9 that it is not his will that any should perish but that all should come to repentance.

It is possible to make a case for the call to come from God in several different ways to everyone who will listen. Has it come to you? Is God calling you to salvation or to some task?

Our saving faith is a source for the spiritual communication mentioned in Romans 8:16 where Paul tells us, "The Spirit himself testifies with our spirit."

The Bible teaches in Hebrews 11:6, "Without faith it is impossible to please God for he rewards those who believe that he is and who diligently seek him. Faith is the power that leads us to the point of repentance and confession resulting in salvation."

When Isaiah uttered those words of agony in the sixth chapter of Isaiah, he was expressing not only his sinful life but also his inability to do anything about it. Even the apostle Paul had his times of frustration. He said in Romans 7:15, "I do not understand what I do. For what I want to do, I do not, but what I hate, I do."

Regardless of all the effort expended, one cannot bring about purity within himself or herself.

That's hard to believe, isn't it? All that is required is confession and repentance. The above scripture makes that abundantly clear. Mercy comes to us when we are convicted and believe that we are sinners, that the unearned mercy of God is available to us and that we are required to express contrition for our sins to the extent that we are willing to confess them and turn from them that Jesus will come into our life and grant salvation; that is a description of saving faith.

Faith provides light that reveals the path to righteousness. There is a simple explanation for the confusion of science and the confidence of Christianity. The difference can be described by one word: faith.

Hebrews 11:1 offers this description of faith: "Now faith is being sure of what we hope for and certain of what we do not see."

In the first part of Hebrews 11:6, the Bible says, "Without faith, it is impossible to please God." Hebrews 11:3 points out the power and the preciousness of faith: "By faith, we understand that the universe was formed at God's command, so that what is seen was not made out of what was visible."

Our faith is a gift from God. Although we have stated the necessity of faith in salvation and described to some extent what it is, the source for the drawing power of faith must be explained.

Because Jesus Christ is our Savior and Lord, it is his desire, purpose, and function to provide a way for our cleansing and ultimately our salvation. He has chosen us because of his grace; he has even provided a vehicle to draw us to the knowledge and awareness of the faith we have been discussing. He informs us that the Holy Spirit is that vehicle: "But I tell you the truth: It is for your good that I am going away. Unless I go away, the counselor will not come to you; but if I go, I will send him to you. When he comes, he will convict the world of guilt in regard to sin and righteousness and judgment: in regard to sin because men do not believe in me; in regard to righteousness, because I am going to the Father, where you can see me no longer; and in regard to judgment, because the prince of this world now stands condemned." (17)

The conviction spoken of in this passage is the beginning of the desire for faith and knowledge; that desire leads one to search for answers. Paul explained the process this way: "Consequently, faith comes from hearing the message, and the message is heard through the word of Christ." (Romans 10:17).

Since salvation is a gift from God, then it must be true that even our faith is provided by him as an act of grace. Someone has said, "Faith is the rocking chair we ride around in while doing God's work." But I believe and the Bible actually teaches that faith is also the vehicle we ride in to accept salvation. Ephesians 2:8–9 carries that communication out a little bit further, elaborates it, and confirms it by saying: "For it is by grace you have been saved, through faith, and that not of yourselves. It is a gift from God—not by works so that no one can boast." Faith provides the strength and the motivation to move forward into acceptance of the offered salvation.

Faith is a departure from the known into the unknown. It is "Walking to the edge of light and taking one more step." Hebrews

11:1 informs us, "Now faith is the assurance of things we hope for, the certainty of things we cannot see."

As we study the word of God and become aware of the great things he has done and witness his great and immeasurable power and love, faith begins to take root and grow to the point that recognizes the past as reality, and we begin to take that step into the darkness some have called ignorance.

Our first step of faith must see him as Lord and creator. When we see him as the powerful God who created heaven and earth that's the beginning of our faith. Hebrews 11:3 informs us: "By faith, we understand that the universe was formed at God's command."

The Bible clearly teaches creation and faith brings us to believe Genesis 1:1 when it says: "In the beginning, God created the heavens and the earth."

When we believe the Bible and the history presented in it, we are convinced of those truths by the power of our faith. The writer of Hebrews 11:2 offers support for our faith when he says: "This is what the ancients were commended for."

The power for our faith comes from recognizing the crucifixion as real. Historians and geologists confirm the scriptural account as it is recorded in Acts 10:39, "They killed him by hanging him on a tree." History confirms it by pointing out that crucifixion was the method of execution used in that era. (18)

As part of the crucifixion experience, the gospels point out that there was a darkness that came over the land during which there were earthquakes, certain individuals rising from the dead, and other unique happenings. Matthew gives this account: "And when Jesus had cried again with a loud voice, he gave up his Spirit. And, behold, the veil of the temple was rent in twain from the top to the bottom; and the earth did quake, and the rocks rent; and the graves were opened; and many bodies of the saints which slept arose, and came out of the graves after his resurrection, and went into the holy city, and appeared unto many. Now when the centurion, and they that were with him, watching Jesus, saw the earthquake, and those things that were done, they feared greatly, saying, truly this was the Son of God. And many women were there beholding afar off, which followed Jesus from Galilee, ministering unto him." Among which were Mary Magdalene, and Mary the mother of James and Jesus, and the mother of Zebedee's children. (19)

Instead of the earthquake and other activity pointed out in Matthew, Luke takes another route and points out the darkness talked about by historians and says: "The first reference we found outside of the Bible mentioning this darkness which fell over the land during the crucifixion of Christ comes from a Samaritan historian named Thallus, who wrote around 52 AD His work was quoted by another early historian by the name of Julius Africanus who researched the topic of this darkness and wrote the following: 'Upon the whole world there came a most fearful darkness. Many rocks were split in two by an earthquake, and many places in Judea and other districts were thrown down. It seems very unreasonable to me that Thallus, in the third book of his histories, would try to explain away this darkness as an eclipse of the sun. For the Jews celebrate their Passover on the fourteenth day according to the moon, and the death of our Savior falls on the day before the Passover. But an eclipse of the sun can only take place when the moon comes under the sun, how then could an eclipse have occurred when the moon is directly opposite the sun? (Scientifically it is impossible to have a full moon on the same day that there is an eclipse of the sun.)'" (20)

It is so very important to accept the reality of that event because the reason for his death on the cross was for you and for me. He became us on that cross. Romans 6:23 tells us, "The wages of sin is death." The cross was the vehicle used for punishing criminals who deserved the death penalty in those days; Jesus died like a criminal. He was executed for the crime of sin; not his sin, because he had no sin. The apostle Paul informs us that: "God made him who had no sin to be sin for us, so in him we might become the righteousness of God" (2 Corinthians 5:21).

Geologists say Jesus, as described in the New Testament, was most likely crucified on Friday, April 3, in the year 33. (By Jennifer Viegas of Discovery News, as reported on NBC News.) (21)

Wow! That gives evidence, if evidence were needed, that the crucifixion of Jesus can be historically and geologically verified. So there it is. The rest of Romans 6:23 informs us: "The gift of God is eternal life through Jesus Christ His Son." He became our proxy there on that cross. "He (that is God) hath made him to be sin for us, who knew no sin; that we might be made the righteousness of God in him" (2 Corinthians 5:21). His blood was shed to wash away our sins—yours and mine.

If the crucifixion were the end of it all, it would be a very sad story. But it is just the beginning chapter in the story of his death and subsequent resurrection because three days later, he arose from the grave. Wow! What a victory! He's not dead! He lives. You ask me how I know he lives; he lives within my heart by the power of faith. It is by the power of saving faith that we recognize the resurrection as real. All four of the gospels tell of the resurrection, every writer of the New Testament writes about it, several of the prophets point toward it during Old Testament times, and now it's here, Paul points out the recording of the event in the scriptures while relating his own experience to the church in Corinth: "That he was buried, that he was raised on the third day according to the Scriptures" (1 Corinthians 15:4). Paul goes even farther than his own personal testimony. He says: "He was seen of above five hundred brethren at once, of whom the greater part remain unto the present, but some are fallen asleep. After that he was seen of James; then of all the apostles. And last of all he was seen of me also, as one born out of due time." (22)

Did you hear what Paul said? He said, "Go ask some of 'em—they're still around. Don't just take my word for it." And I say with him, "Don't take my word for it; you can know through the power of saving faith."

Power for Our Faith Is Provided When We Recognize the Ascension as Real

Luke 24:51 informs us, "While he was blessing them, he left them and was taken up into heaven."

It is more difficult to document the ascension because just a few of his followers were present, but we can attest to the validity when

LIGHTING THE PATH OF RIGHTEOUSNESS

we consider the evidence presented for his crucifixion and subsequent resurrection. But the belief of its authenticity really is a matter of faith.

If you have made up your mind and have ignored the evidence and the call from God, no amount of historical facts will convince you anyway. The apostle Paul makes a very pertinent point, however, in 1 Corinthians 15:14, when he says, "And if Christ has not been raised, our preaching is useless and so is your faith."

Power For Our Faith Is Provided When We Recognize the Presence of Jesus In and Among Us

Light provided by our faith makes it possible for us to accept the word of Jesus as evidence of his presence. It enables us to follow the example of the father spoken about in John 4:50. Scripture informs us that when Jesus heard his plea for help: "Jesus replied 'You may go. Your son will live.'"

Watch the audacity of this man's faith. The life of his son is on the line. Surely one could expect Jesus to have the courtesy to go to his house and speak to his son; maybe even lay hands upon him but the man took Jesus at his word and departed.

The Bible says, "God has chosen the simple to confound the wise." Are you one of those who would complicate the simple word of Jesus, or are you one of those who considers himself wise and saved?

The Light Provided By Our Faith Allows Us To Experience the Spiritual Presence of Jesus In Our Midst

Are we back to the point we talked about earlier concerning spiritual communication? It's worth repeating and remembering because that's one of the ways we know we have been saved. 1 John 3:24 emphatically makes this point: "Those who obey his commands live in him, and he in them." I believe it would be safe to say that no one is obedient to the will and word of God all the time, but there is an attitude that brings forth that effort and the desire for repentance and forgiveness when we fail; That's why John informs us that: if we sin "we have an advocate with the Father, Jesus Christ the righteous" (1 John 2:1, KJV).

"And this is how we know that he lives in us. We know it by the Spirit he gave us."

Because Christians have been called out and born again into the kingdom of God, we believe his promises. One of those promises is that of his spiritual presence. In Matthew 18:20, we are informed of that presence: "For where two or three come together in my name, there am I with them." But more than that, he has promised that presence all the time for all our life time. He completed his great commission statement in the last part of Matthew 28:20 by saying, "And surely I am with you, to the very end of the age."

Light is provided for our faith when we see the present as a time to prepare for the future. One of the most precious hymns I know is "Because He Lives." Some of the words are: "Because he lives, I can face tomorrow." That is true because our faith makes it possible. Hebrews 12:1 reminds us of our commitment to progress in the gospel and says: "Therefore, since we are surrounded by such a great cloud of witnesses, let us throw off everything that hinders and the sin that so easily entangles, and let us run with perseverance the race that is marked out for us."

Hope provides power for our faith that enables us to prepare for the future. The writer of the book of Hebrews tells us, "Now faith is being sure of what we hope for and certain of what we do not see" (Hebrews 11:1).

There is a story told by Chester E. Shuler many years ago about a little boy who was flying his kite.

"The wind was strong and it soared upward in a way to delight any lad's heart. Finally, it had vanished entirely from sight.

A gentleman came along and noticed the boy hanging onto the strong cord which anchored the kite to earth.

"What are you doing, son?" he asked, smiling.

"Flying my kite," answered the little boy proudly.

"Your kite? But I can't see any kite."

"It's up there, sir—way up out of sight!" declared the boy.

"How do you know it's up there?"

"I can feel it tug, mister! That's how I know it" was the apt answer.

Shortly afterward, this Christian man met an infidel. A discussion of religion ensued because the infidel never lost an opportunity to try to undermine some Christian's faith, if possible.

"You believe in God?" he said, laughing lightly. "Well, I don't see how you know there's a God up there in heaven."

"I know it by the spirit, my friend," the Christian replied. Then remembering the kite incident, he quickly added, "I can feel the tug of heaven and God. I know they are up there!" (23)

Spiritual light provides power to our faith for daily living. Romans 8:37 says, "We are more than conquerors through him who loved us."

Spiritual light reveals that life eternal is available to all who trust him and call upon his holy name. Paul offers this promise concerning everlasting life for the believer: "For the Lord, himself will come down from heaven with a loud command, with the voice of an archangel and with the trumpet call of God, and the dead in Christ will rise first, after that we who are still alive and are left will be caught up together with them in the clouds to meet the Lord in the air." (24)

Because of that hope, we look forward to the return of Jesus. The disciples watched in awe, amazement and consternation as Jesus ascended into heaven but angels came and offered them this assurance: "Men of Galilee, they said, why do you stand here looking up into the sky? This same Jesus who has been taken from you into heaven will come back in the same way you have seen him go into heaven."

Spiritual light provides spiritual communication as proof of salvation.

Conversion was never portrayed more vividly than in the conversions of Paul and Isaiah.

Because of his experience, Paul could say, "The Spirit himself testifies with our spirit that we are God's children" (Romans 8:16).

Although in a different, and perhaps a more or less dramatic way than the apostle Paul but just as real, that act of conversion was true with Isaiah in the temple and to the Philippian jailor and so it should be, to one extent or another, with everyone who undergoes an authentic conversion. Look at Saul wallowing in the dirt on the road to Damascus. He asked the question many believe he already knew the answer to: "Who are you Lord" (Acts 9:5). Jesus answered his question and gave him instructions

A preacher asked me some time ago if Saul had a choice. Maybe the answer is yes and no. If you want to argue with someone who has appeared to you in a bright light, knocked you to the ground and blinded you, all I can say is go ahead.

After Saul received his instructions, had his eyes opened miraculously and had eaten, and was baptized he was ready to go to work. "At once he began to preach in the synagogues that Jesus is the Son of God" (Acts 9:20).

When Phillip was instructed by the Holy Spirit to approach the Ethiopian Eunuch, there was no hesitation: "Go south to the road—the desert road—that goes down from Jerusalem to Gaza so he started out" (Acts 8:26–28).

I have often wondered how some people can get so excited they jump up and down at a ball game but show very little excitement at the great news of salvation.

It has been my experience, and apparently that of others, when Jesus becomes a part of our life, we must witness. I can identify with the words of Jeremiah: "But if I say, 'I will not mention him or speak anymore in his name, his word is in my heart like a fire, a fire shut up in my bones, I am weary of holding it in, indeed I cannot'" (Jeremiah 20:9).

The words of John echo the same refrain: "This we proclaim concerning the Word of Life" (1 John1:1).

Jesus told those who were witnesses of his departure: "Therefore, go and make disciples of all nations, baptizing them in the name of the Father and of the Son and of the Holy Spirit" (Matthew 28:19). In Acts, he told them again in a slightly different way: "But you will receive power when the Holy Spirit comes on you; and you will be my witnesses" (Acts 1:8).

The verses designated by many as "The great commission" are verses that direct us to "proclaim." John said, "We proclaim to you what we have seen and heard" (1 John 1:3).

Churches are dwindling away across America and pastors huddle in an effort to solve the problem. No football game has ever been won in the huddle! I can give you what I see as the solution: get back to the Bible. You know those verses that say, "Go tell" and "Ye shall be witnesses of me," etc.

It is true that political correctness and government rules have caused many restrictions on the church, but we have a choice. We can huddle in the upper room or we can "go teach all nations." How are you reacting to the restrictions placed on the church by the world and the government? Can others see Jesus in you? If they can't, maybe he really isn't there.

Spiritual light reveals a physical relationship that is proof of a Christian experience. The Christian experience is a fellowship with other Christians: "We proclaim to you what we have seen and heard, so that you may have fellowship with us" (1 John 1:3). After Jesus ascended into heaven, a hundred twenty of his followers assembled in an upper room (Acts 1:15). After his crucifixion, the twelve assembled in a room. When Peter was thrown into prison, Christians came together in the house of Mary, the mother of John for a prayer meeting (Acts 12:12).

The writer of Hebrews tells us: "Let us not give up the assembling of ourselves together as some are in the habit of doing, but let us encourage one another" (Hebrews 10:25).

As a personal testimony, I would say there have been times when I have been tempted to drop out of church because of discouragement or abuse, but I couldn't do it. God would not let me be comfortable until I went back to church.

A young man in New Mexico was very enthusiastic about witnessing. On several occasions, he spoke of witnessing to people in the line at some market or some other event, but he was disappointed when they didn't come to church. There is a vast difference between saying a "little prayer" and having a personal experience with Christ Jesus. After all confession is only part of the plan of salvation. Paul said: "That if you confess with your mouth (that's part of it) "Jesus is Lord and believe in your heart God raised him from the dead, you will be saved" (Romans 10:9).

Talk is cheap. I once considered myself a bronc rider and said I could ride some of toughest broncs in the world, but I was thrown from a young colt six times in about thirty minutes one morning. It is important to realize that salvation is a change of heart, a change of mind, and a change of behavior. Paul said: "For it is with your heart that you believe and are justified, and it is with your mouth that you confess and are saved" (Romans 10:10). Paul told the Ephesians: "For we are God's workmanship, created to do good works, which God has prepared for us to do" (Ephesians 2:10).

It is my understanding and experience that if you are really saved, you will want to be with other Christians; you will want that fellowship for the strength it provides and the comfort that should be available in time of need.

The Christian experience is fellowship with God. John says, "And our hands have touched" (1 John 1:1c). He tells his listeners their relationship is continuing even to the day of his writing to them and says, "And our fellowship is with the Father" (1 John 1:3b).

I can't even begin to remember the times I have heard someone say, "I want to join the church" or "I joined the church today." The question comes immediately—did they join the fellowship of true believers in Christ or just become a recorded member of the church group?

Please don't misunderstand the importance or the availability of salvation! Peter tells us: "He is patient with you, not wanting anyone to perish, but everyone to come to repentance" (2 Peter 3:9), but it is necessary to come to a saving realization of Christ in your life before you "join the church" and he has made that possible by his amazing grace. Since that is true, the question must be asked—if it isn't his will that you should perish, then whose will is it? This fellowship with the father can be a time of comfort for he is, "The God of all comfort." It can be a source of strength. It can even be a source of genuine joy.

The Christian experience is one of joy. There is certainly joy in fellowship with other Christians found through being a part of a group who has many things in common. John informed the recipients of his letter: "We write this to make your joy complete" (1 John 1:4). To be a part of this fellowship, you must have Jesus as your Lord and Savior.

Because the church is a body of baptized believers in Christ Jesus, if you are not saved, you are not a part of the fellowship. You might mingle with them and be friendly with them, but Jesus points out: "Goats do not share the same destination as sheep" (Matthew 25:25–31).

One morning in a little Baptist church in Alabama, one of the deacons was asked to pray. His whole prayer was about gratefulness to God for being in church with his friends and relatives. It is true there is great satisfaction from being in church with friends and relatives, but for me at least, the greatest of all joys is the joy of fellowship with God.

One might hear someone say, "I'm just not happy being a Christian anymore," or some phrase to that effect. We are not talking about happiness. There is a great difference between joy and happiness. Happiness is defined in the *New World Dictionary* as "favored by circumstances; lucky, fortunate; having, showing, or causing a feeling of great pleasure." (25) From that definition, one can deduce that *happiness* is caused by an external environment.

Joy, on the other hand, is defined by the same dictionary as "a very glad feeling: happiness or great pleasure; delight, anything causing such a feeling." (26) The difference between the definitions of these two words would be one—joy is the source of happiness but happiness is also caused by circumstances.

Baker's Dictionary of Theology states: "The NT regards joy essentially a divine bestowal." (27) It is with that statement in mind we discuss Christian joy and, apparently, what John had in mind when he said, "We write this to make your joy complete" (1 John 1:4).

Author, pastor, and evangelist John Macarthur describes joy this way in his commentary on Philippians:

> Most people define happiness as an attitude of satisfaction or delight based on circumstances largely beyond their control. Spiritual joy, on the other hand, is deep and abiding confidence that regardless of one's circumstance in life, all is well with the believer in God. (28)

Knowing that God has saved us by his grace through our faith always brings joy to us. Who among us cannot identify with the writer of Psalms 4:7 when he exclaims in his cry to God: "You have put gladness in our heart." There are more than two hundred references to joy in the bible, in all its forms. From these references and the awareness in our own life, that joy is indeed part of God's plan for Christians and it is found through full fellowship with him

CHAPTER 2

The World of Light

1 John 1:5, 7, 9

In the world of light, God is the light.

When we returned from a mission in Vietnam one evening after dark, we pivoted in a circle with our landing light and our search light on to determine if we had unwanted company. (29)

Those lights would brighten up every place they shined, but there were still shadows. There was a contrast between the shadows and the places the light touched.

John informs us that "God is light" (1 John 1:5). With him, there is no shadow because he not only is the source of light. He is light.

Because there is no darkness in the world of light, all the glory of God is revealed.

In the ninth chapter of Acts, Paul was struck down by that light. Although it was around noon, the light he saw was much brighter than the sun. He describes it to Festus as "a light from heaven, brighter than the sun, blazing around me and my companions" (Acts 26:13).

Because of the brightness and the all-encompassing ability of God's light, all we are and do is revealed. In that revelation, all true Christians are recognized as the, "Light of the world" (Matthew 5:14)

Spiritual Light Is Available Through Various Sources

The Bible is the primary source for spiritual light. Paul admonished Timothy to: "Study to show thyself approved, a workman that needeth not to be ashamed, rightly dividing the word of truth" (1 Timothy 2:15 KJV). The NIV words it a little differently but reflects the same call for commitment: "Do your best to present yourself to God as one approved, a workman who does not need to be ashamed and who correctly handles the word of truth."

Most of us deplore willful ignorance in the field of worldly knowledge such as math, mechanics, etc. Ignorance of the word of God should be just as deplorable in the Christian world.

Some have been heard to say, "I don't read the Bible because I can't understand it." It is true that much of the Bible is beyond our comprehension, but much of it, the part we need to know, the part God wants us to know, can be opened to us by the power of the Holy Spirit through prayer and diligent study.

That power is available to every one of us by spiritual light who have received Christ as our Savior and who pray and talk with him regularly. Paul confirms the availability of that power by saying: "Now we have received not the spirit of the world, but the Spirit which is of God, that we might know the things that are freely given us by the Holy Spirit who is from God" (1 Corinthians 2:12).

In the world of light too many of us are waiting and wishing for something or someone to tell us what we want or need to know or do. The dominant philosophy seems to expect everything to be done to us or for us. Jesus made it clear that Christianity is not that kind of lifestyle. It's just a fact; you can't catch fish in the desert. If you want to experience the light of Jesus Christ in your life, it is imperative that appropriate action is taken.

That action must begin with searching the scriptures. One of the recommended ways to do that is to set a regular time aside for Bible study.

During that time of study, spend time in prayer. Prayer is defined as a conversation with God. That conversation could, and should, include thanksgiving, petition for others, and forgiveness for sin, as well as other subjects.

Go into the world with a Bible in your hand, the glory of God on your heart, and the Word of God in your mouth.

If you want vegetables from your garden, you need to go to the garden to get them. By the same token, if you want a closer walk with Jesus, time spent studying God's word is the road to that experience.

Jesus tells us in Matthew 16:24, "If anyone would come after me, he must take up his cross and follow me." Yet how can one follow if the way is unclear? Making that path clear and open is the purpose for lighting the path of righteousness

It seems some are plaintively crying, "Pastor, bring me a cross." Get your own cross! Better still, take up the cross of Jesus and follow him. As you do, your enlightenment will increase, you will grow in faith and in grace, and you will begin to enjoy your Christianity.

Many who claim ignorance of the Bible, and consequently the will and way of God, struggle because they are not regularly exposed to the environment where learning occurs. That is a function of the local church.

While it is true that witnessing is a necessary part of being a Christian, by the same token, you can't get water from an empty well; attending church and Bible study whenever they are available fills that well of knowledge and blesses the receiver. If you want to learn about God, you need to go where God's people are regularly found. Hebrews 10:24–25 offers this advice:

> Let us consider how we may spur one another
> on toward love and good deeds. Let us not give
> up meeting together, as some are in the habit of
> doing, but let us encourage one another, and all
> the more as you see the day approaching. (30)

The world of light is made available relative to our ability to comprehend. Do you remember those bottles used for Rose Hair Oil? Maybe you used some other brand you had to turn the bottle upside down and shake it to get the oil out. Perhaps your favorite "hair oil" had a different name.

Do you remember how hard it was to get the liquids from those bottles with the tiny holes in the top? This illustration is an indicator of my age; perhaps you are much younger, but you might be able to identify with the illustration of a tiny opening. Have you ever tried pouring liquid back in a container with a tiny opening? I'm probably the only one in the world who would try such a thing. It is an attempt at a near impossibility without the knowledge and the right equipment. Have you ever tried to teach someone like that? They were so closed minded, they refused to accept the information you were presenting. Paul informed the church at Ephesus that he was praying for them about that very thing.

> That Christ may dwell in your hearts by faith, and I pray for you, that you being rooted and established in love, may have power together with all the saints, to grasp how wide and how long and how deep is the love of Christ. (31).

Jesus said, "Blessed are those who hunger and thirst for righteousness, for they will be filled" (Matthew 5:6). That hunger and that thirst is an integral part of the makeup of every authentic Christian. It is driven by the desire that they might be filled with the presence of God. That can only happen when our heart is filled with authentic humility and we are ready to submit to his leadership and teaching.

If you are too busy thirsting after the things of the world, then you need to examine the authenticity of your "conversion."

A saying I have concocted for myself, or picked up somewhere makes a lot of sense to me, "You can't pour liquid in a full glass." The individual who is full of worldly dreams and activities and has no desire to seek after the things of God will someday stand before the judgment seat to explain why he or she had no time for Jesus.

In the world of light the path to righteousness is revealed by its definition. As we consider a discussion concerning God as light, we need to understand the definition and meaning of light as it is used in the scriptures. *Easton's Illustrated Bible Dictionary* informs us:

> Light came naturally to typify true religion and the felicity it imparts (Psalm 119:105; Isaiah 8:20; Matthew 4:16) and the glorious inheritance of the redeemed (Colossians 1:12; Revelation 21:23–15). In its highest sense, it is applied to Christ as the, "Sun of righteousness" (Malachi 4:2; Luke 2:32; John 1:7–9). (32)

It is no wonder Paul was struck down by it, or that Isaiah was struck with awareness of his sinfulness. That same brightness shines through all pretense and causes us to look at our self as we really are.

Everyone is blemished with the marks of sin. Darkness hides those blemishes and makes it easy to ignore their existence, but the light from the "sun of righteousness" will cause every blemish to stand out in dark contrast to the perfection of righteousness. We are taught from the Bible that God knows us to the very depth of our innermost beings; consequently, pretense is utterly futile and destructive.

We are informed by John: "If we claim to have fellowship with him yet walk in darkness, we lie and do not the truth" (1 John 1:6). It is possible to deceive others, even ourselves. In 1 John 1:8, we find this truth: "If we claim to be without sin, we deceive ourselves and the truth is not in us." I suppose it is possible to believe that John is addressing certain individuals, but the apostle Paul completely discounts that possibility when he says, "For all have sinned and fall short of the glory of God" (Romans 3:23). That is one of the reasons for this effort.

It is possible to know if we know God or if we are living in deception. It is my prayer if you are confused or unsure, that certainty can be determined through much prayer and examination of this work and others concerning salvation

Recognition of sin and inadequacy is only a prelude to the greatest revelation of all. That is the revelation of Jesus Christ as the light that is salvation. That light has three qualities to consider as it works in our life. It has drawing power, it has cleansing power, and it has saving power.

Spiritual light has drawing power. The light that draws us to salvation has its source in the love of God. In Jeremiah 31:3, we find these words of assurance: "The Lord appeared to us in the past, saying, 'I have loved you with an everlasting love; I have drawn you with loving—kindness.'"

These words of encouragement can be found in 1 John 3:1: "How great is the love the Father has lavished on us, that we should be called the children of God!"

The apostle Paul ties that love to the light when he says, "For God who said, 'Let light shine out of darkness,' made his light shine in our hearts to give us the light of the knowledge of the glory of God in the face of Christ" (2 Corinthians 4:6).

Evidence of the drawing power of that shining light is exemplified by the writer of Psalms 42:1 with these words, "As a deer pants for streams of water, so my soul pants for You, O God."

Spiritual light has cleansing power. The cleansing power found in the world of light is found in the desire of every true Christian to be like Jesus. There have been songs and hymns beyond number concerning this desire. It is part of the proof of salvation.

Jesus said to his disciples, and to us, "If you love me, you will obey what I command" (John 14:15). Does this mean if you are disobedient, you are lost? Not necessarily; we are clearly taught that no one is perfect, but I believe it is impossible to be saved and not love Jesus. Obedience is an indication of loyalty and loyalty to Christ would mean cleaning up any faults, shortcomings, or known sin in your life and following Jesus because of our love for him.

Spiritual light has saving power. The saving power found in the world of light is the light that reveals Jesus himself. Jesus said: "I am the way, the truth, and the life. No one comes to the Father but through me" (John 14:6).

John informs us: "But if we walk in the light, as he is in the light, we have fellowship with one another, and the blood of Jesus Christ, his Son, purifies us from all sin" (1 John 1:7). He is the path to righteousness. He is the light that draws us to him. He is the light that cleanses us from unrighteousness. He is the light that saves us from everlasting destruction. He is the saving light.

In the World of Light for Salvation is Revealed, the way of salvation conditions are revealed.

There is the condition of confession. 1 John 1:9a makes that very clear with the promise that, "If we confess our sins he is faithful and just to forgive us our sins and will purify us from all unrighteousness."

Webster's New World Dictionary informs us that, "The word confession means acknowledgment or an admission of guilt; consequently, there can be no such thing as secret Christians." (33) In the Christian world confession means telling others or telling Jesus. Since we are all sinners by biblical definition, confession is required for forgiveness by everyone.

There is the faithfulness of God to be recognized, "He is faithful and just" (1 John 1:9b).

Forgiveness is not given because of our merit or standing. I once heard a preacher relate how one of his members was "rescued from death." He had the audacity to describe how, he had told God about this person being a good Sunday school teacher, a good tither and other attributes, then demanded God to heal her. What audacity!

Isaiah tells us, "Our righteousness is as filthy rags." Although we are told in Hebrews to approach the throne of grace boldly, that doesn't mean we are in charge over the one true and sovereign God. We have no right or power to persuade God to forgive us, all we can do is to confess our sins and our inadequacies then, because of his faithfulness and because of his sense of justice and his amazing grace, he decides on his merit and because of his mercy, to forgive us.

There is a completion of cleansing. 1 John 1:9c informs us he will "forgive us our sins and purify (cleanse) us from all unrighteousness." Isaiah speaks for God to the Israelites and says, "'Come now, let us reason together,' says the Lord, 'Though your sins be like scarlet, they shall be white as snow, though they are as red as crimson, they shall be as wool'" (Isaiah1:18). Wow! What a promise

CHAPTER 3

The World of Darkness

1 John 1:6, 8, 10; 2:1

The *World Book Encyclopedia* reveals this startling fact, "Most kinds (of fishes) living in caves are quite blind. (34) Do they know they are blind? Who would know? Is it even relevant? Is it reasonable to compare their situation with those who are lost?"

In several places the Bible compares being lost to ignorance or darkness and those who have been saved as: "Walking in the light. John informs us that, God is light; in him there is no darkness at all" (1 John 1:5). The Apostle Paul tells the Christians at Ephesus, "For you were once darkness but now you are light in the Lord; live as children of light" (Ephesians 5:8).

The Bible points out a reason for being concerned about whether we walk in darkness or light or even worse, pretending to be in the light when we live in darkness. We are informed by John:

> If we claim to have fellowship with him yet walk
> in darkness, we lie and do not live by the truth.
> But if we walk in the light, as he is in the light, we
> have fellowship with one another, and the blood
> of Jesus his Son, purifies us from all sin. (35)

In his letter to the Colossians, Paul seems to suggest the existence of two different (spiritual) worlds when he says, "For he has rescued us from the dominion of darkness and brought us into the kingdom of the Son he loves" (Colossians 1:13). I understand that to be equivalent to the two worlds addressed in 1 John as the worlds of darkness and light.

The World of Darkness Is a World of Ignorance

Several commentators have concluded that one of the reasons John wrote his first epistle was to combat heresy within the church which lead to ignorance of the grace of God uplifted a pursuit of knowledge in its place. *The New Commentary on The Whole Bible* offers this opinion, "One of the reasons that prompted his first epistle was that a heretical faction had developed within the Church." (36)

Adam Clarke's Commentary states, "That the design of this epistle was to combat the doctrine delivered by certain false teachers appears from 1 John 2:18–26; 1 John 3:7 and what this false doctrine was may be inferred from the counter doctrine delivered by St John, 1 John 5:1–6." (37)

Donald Guthrie, in his book on New Testament Theology, points out that, "Although Plato did not go as far as the Gnostics in regarding all matter as evil, he nevertheless considered that the body was a mass of evil." (38)

Many commentaries identify the group called Gnostics with a high level of certainty as the group or philosophy John was dealing with.

John further addresses the claim of the Gnostics with this statement claiming authenticity is indicated by fidelity: "If we claim to have fellowship with him and walk in darkness, we lie and do not live by the truth" (1 John 1:6).

The message found in 1 John 2:3–10 makes the point of the need for authenticity even more salient. In those verses John makes it clear, that obedience is evidence of salvation. He makes it very clear that proof of authentic salvation is observed in those who walk the walk of obedience: "We know that we have come to know him if we obey his commands" (1 John 2:3).

True obedience is more than just following orders or direction. Guy H. King advances the very pertinent point that it is a matter of the heart, head, and lifestyle by pointing out:

> As John records in chapter xv, of his gospel, Our Lord chose a very familiar process of nature in order to press home the fundamental necessity of the believer to abide in him. (39)

In John 14:15 Jesus said, "If anyone loves me, he will obey my commands."

A story is told of a little boy who was not sitting in his seat at school. The teacher asked him to sit in his seat several times but he just stood and looked at her; finally, she demanded that he sit or receive disciplinary action. He sat down but muttered under his breath, "I'm still standing up in my head." (40)

That is not true obedience. True and authentic obedience is unconditional and total surrender. Jesus made that apparent when he told his disciples: "If anyone would come after me, he must deny himself and take up his cross and follow me" (Matthew 16:24).

There is an obvious difference in the behavior of those who are in the army and those who made the army their career. In my twenty years as a soldier in the US Army, I observed individuals who were unwilling participants in military things and individuals who had adapted their attitude and their behavior to reflect that being a soldier was more than an occupation.

For those who considered the army a way of life, that attitude was reflected in attitude and behavior. Many of those who have retired or gotten out for some other reason still maintain the attitude and mannerisms of a soldier. Those people could be considered fanatics.

You possibly know someone you consider a fanatical Christian. Allow me to ask if you are a sports fan. Perhaps you are a fan of football or maybe basketball? The word *fan* is an abbreviation of the word fanatic. I have known people who lived and breathed sports—sort of.

They could tell you yardage, interceptions, touchdowns, RBIs, and strikeouts—even the size and weight of the players; but you seldom heard them talk about Jesus. I'm sorry to say some of those individuals called themselves pastors and preachers.

Yes! I'm a Jesus fan. I know very little sports. I performed very poorly in that area while attending school because of poverty and inconvenience, but I am a Jesus fan. I surrendered to Jesus many years ago, when I was still a little boy. That doesn't mean I haven't strayed or brought shame to his precious name. I have, but in my insufficient and haphazard way I have surrendered to him.

My Bible teaches that salvation is unconditional surrender. John confirms that need when he says: "But if anyone obeys his word, God's love is truly made complete in him" (1 John 2:5).

Obedience involves conversion; conversion means change. Jesus said, "I tell you the truth: no one can see the kingdom of God unless he is born again" (John 3:3).

J. Vernon McGee makes this comment about conversion: "You can bluff your way through but you cannot have that deep, down-in-your-heart assurance unless you keep his commandments." (41)

Have you ever known someone who claimed to be a Christian but kept it well hidden by his or her lifestyle?

I was acquainted with a young man who aspired to leadership in a church where I was pastor several years ago. I went to his job one day for some reason and found him telling a dirty joke with profuse profanity involved. I tried to talk to him about it. His response was, "I have to talk like that so they will like me." It was, and is, my opinion that his problem was much deeper than lack of popularity. (42)

He is not the first or only person who has made a profession of faith then denied its authenticity by their behavior. John has a description for those people. He says, "The man who says, 'I know him.' but does not do his commands is a liar and the truth is not in him" (1 John 2:4).

Jesus makes this statement about such people, "By their fruit you will recognize them. Do people pick grapes from thorn bushes or figs from thistles" (Matthew 7:16).

Jesus described authentic disciples, as salt and light and reminded them of the need for authenticity when he said: "You are the salt of the earth. But if the salt loses its saltiness, how can it be made salty again? It is no longer good for anything except to be thrown out and trampled by men; you are the light of the world. A city on a hill cannot be hidden." (43)

Some Individuals who Live in Darkness Are Ignorant of Their Ignorance

Jesus referred to the ignorance of those of Noah's day, "For in the days before the flood people were eating and drinking, marrying and giving in marriage until the day Noah entered the ark and they knew nothing about what would happen until the flood came and took them away." As an example of the need for authentic faith. (44)

From this statement, like the blind fish, previously mentioned, who live in caves, it appears that the people of Noah's day were ignorant of the fact that they were ignorant.

I would like to describe this as innocent darkness. It seems to me that many lost people don't realize they live in a world of darkness and because of this ignorance they really aren't concerned about their everlasting future.

Some Individuals who Live in Darkness Are Ignorant of Their Final Destination

This state of ignorance and the danger of it is pointed out in Matthew 24:39, "And they knew nothing until the flood came and took them all away."

As I drove to church this morning, I heard a preacher point out the deterioration of Christianity. As I was driving home from church this afternoon, I heard another preacher warning of the waning influence of Christianity. The latter preacher blamed it on the pastors and preachers of America. His words of warning were directed toward those "who are in the pulpits of America." I can agree. Of the several local churches I have attended in search of one who is friendly, Christ centered and evangelistic, I have yet to find one.

As we seek proof of our Christian experience, let's begin by looking at the world of darkness. It is not difficult to establish the premise that many of those who live in a world of darkness also live in a world of ignorance. The Adam Clark Commentary makes this statement concerning a world of darkness: "Darkness implies all imperfection, and principally ignorance, sinfulness, and misery." (45)

While reading a book written by Harold T. Bryson titled *Increasing the Joy*, the thought came to mind, "That sounds like the world we're living in now." He said: "Paganism was rampant in the first century. Vicious corruption, extending to every aspect of life, was the pagan world's hallmark. Lust, avarice, bribery, pleasures, and disdain for human life were socially acceptable. Honesty, chastity, compassion, and unpretentious living were disdained. Believers had a difficult time because the world was so degraded." (46)

All that could be said of the world today with one exception; much of the corruption is tolerated or encouraged by many of our contemporary churches.

One example of that degradation is the celebration of Easter. Easter is a holiday many churches prepare for in a big way. Some churches plan a concert or a pageant, and that's great; but others plan "Easter egg hunts to attract the children in the community." If you see this in a positive way, or if you are one of those who are doing it, allow me to explain the celebration and source of Easter egg hunts.

First allow me to establish the source of the word *Easter* as it is defined in the *The World Book Encyclopedia*, "Easter takes its name in English from that of an Anglo-Saxon goddess, Eostre, who represented light in, or spring. The Anglo-Saxon tribes held a festival in her honor every April. Easter eggs are a sign (symbol) of new life. Legend has it that they are laid by the Easter rabbit on Easter." (47)

One might say, "I don't see anything wrong with that, it's just a little thing." What happened to the commandment that informs us that we should not worship other gods? "But it's such a small thing."

While serving in the military service in the field of aircraft maintenance, I was reminded many times of the importance of small things. I came very close to crashing in the desert because someone had failed to tighten a fitting on a fuel line. I was almost killed once because someone failed to tighten a nut known to helicopter mechanics as the "Jesus nut."

In that situation, a special crew was conducting a routinely scheduled inspection on a helicopter. There was a big push to get it done as quickly as possible the reason for that big push was that the company commander wanted to break a previous record.

There was a vibration in flight, so it was my duty to ride with the maintenance officer on a test flight after it had been repaired. We flew it several times but never found the problem. The next morning a pilot found the main rotor mast retaining nut holding on by two threads. In their haste, they had failed to tighten one nut. It just happened to be the main rotor mast retaining nut (commonly known as the "Jesus nut" for good reason). It is the nut at the very top of everything. It holds the rotor blades on the helicopter. Without it, the helicopter falls out of the sky like a rock—sort of.

Celebrating pagan holidays with pagan activities is not a little thing. We cannot and should not be competing with the world by mimicking their activities. Our great commission and our mandate are written in Matthew 28:20: "Go into the world and teach the gospel to every creature." I have attempted to discuss outreach with the leaders of some of the churches I have attended. Each time I try to discuss outreach in the community, the suggestion is met with excuses or hostility.

Although there are exceptions, it seems most of the churches I attend are very willing to go to China, Mexico, or India while people are just outside their door dying and going to hell without Christ. The very people they are ignoring and have a primary responsibility for are ignorant and dismissive of their destination, and there are very few in the church who will direct them otherwise.

Although many ignore the claim that the Bible speaks of hell more than it speaks of heaven, it is the other choice. There are those who believe it is possible to buy one of their loved ones out of the clutches of hell. My Bible teaches emphatically, "Just as man is appointed to die once, and after that to face the judgment so Christ was sacrificed once to take away the sins of many people . . ." (Hebrews 9:27).

Regarding those who are lost and following the ways of evil, Jesus described their destination: "Then they will go away to eternal punishment, but the righteous to eternal life" (Matthew 25:46).

Are you ignorant of your destination? You might be one of those who say, as one young lady said to me and a deacon from the church where I was pastor at the time: "I've got a lot of wild oats to sow yet," "Maybe later," or "I'll think about it." She died two weeks later in a car wreck. (49)

If that frightens you, I'm sorry. If it causes you to think about your everlasting destination, I'm glad.

The Bible teaches in at least three different places that, "Every knee will bow." We find this statement in Isaiah: "Before me every knee will bow; by me every tongue will swear" (Isaiah 45:23). The apostle Paul echoes that phrase in his letter to the church in Rome: "As surely as I live, says the Lord, every knee will bow before me; every tongue will confess to God" (Romans 14:11). He repeats the same message in Philippians: "That at the name of Jesus every knee should bow, in heaven and on earth and under the earth" (Philippians 2:10). He goes a step farther and says, "So then, each of us will give an account of himself to God. When that day of accounting comes, those who live in darkness: "Will go away into eternal punishment, but the righteous into eternal life" (Romans 14:12 NKJV).

That is why Jesus declared, "All power is given me in heaven and in earth," followed by our marching orders: "Go ye therefore, and teach all nations, baptizing them in the name of the Father, and the Son, and the Holy Ghost Teaching them to observe all things I have commanded you; and lo, I am with you always, even unto the end of the world. Amen." (50) That's why it's so important to tell others about Jesus.

Some who live in darkness resist the gospel. There is a point to be made concerning resistance to the gospel. These are those who are willingly ignorant and live in darkness. I have been told numerous times, "Religion is supposed to be kept in the church." I have also been ridiculed for my Christianity several times.

When I was stationed in Korea, I was "baptized" with a whisky coke. One night, I had gone to bed early because I found that was one way to avoid trouble. While I was lying in my bunk, I heard voices approaching and I heard one of the young men say, "Let's baptize old Stafford." I just pulled my covers up over my head because I knew it was futile to resist. (51)

Those three young men had heard me try to witness. They had seen me go to chapel every Sunday, and it seemed to offend them. This was their way of resisting the light.

Jesus makes a point in John 3:20 I have seen proven several times: "Everyone who does evil hates the light, and will not come into the light for fear that his deeds will be exposed."

There are exceptions, however, to that rule. One exception I experienced in my ministry occurred several years ago.

While pastor of a church in Kansas, I began witnessing to a man, seventy-six years old, who was considered to have a reputation for "meanness." He eventually came to know the Lord. (52)

It took time and prayer and the drawing power of God, but we baptized him and rejoiced.

There are many others, however, to whom I have witnessed who have rejected the message of salvation. A soldier I worked with at Fort Hood Texas was one of those people.

He dropped in to visit me one night while I was on charge of quarters. That's a military term for one who stays in the company office overnight to answer the phones and do various other duties.

I always took my Bible to read while on duty. We visited a short while, then he picked up my Bible and began to discuss his point-of-view of the Bible and some of the things he believed to be true about it; none of which had anything to do with Christianity.

Eventually, I began to witness to him about salvation. After a few minutes, he became agitated, and before long, he became angry enough to throw my Bible at me. It landed in my stomach and knocked the breath out of me. I still remember his threat quite vividly: "If you know what's good for you, don't come on the flight line tomorrow." Well, you see, I didn't have much choice. I was in the army, and they have a name for people who aren't where they're supposed to be when they're supposed to be there with certain punishments that go with it. Besides, I was his immediate supervisor. So I went to work dreading what might happen. I was pleasantly surprised—he was quite friendly. I regret to say, however, I never had a chance to witness to him again.

It is possible that he lives in darkness to this day. I hope I'm wrong. I have prayed for him often. Only God knows. (53)

It is my conclusion that he loved the world too much. He drank heavily and "celebrated" constantly for real or fabricated reasons with alcohol. He knew his life was a life of sin and he loved sin more than life, therefore, he chose to wander around in his world of darkness.

The World of Darkness Is a World of Negativity and Distrust

Because most of those who live in darkness are surrounded with a sense of insecurity, there is an attitude of distrust of others. Adam Clarke puts it this way: "God is to the human soul what light is to the world; without the latter all would be dismal and uncomfortable, and terror and death would usually prevail." (54)

One possibility is that those who live with an attitude of distrust judge others by their own standards and find them lacking.

Adam Clark tells us in his introduction to the letter of 1 John:

> In the first chapter the four first verses are opposed to the following assertion of the Gnostics: "That the apostles did not deliver the doctrine of Jesus as they had received it, but made additions to it, especially in the commandments which were termed legal; whereof they themselves (the Gnostics) retained the genuine and uncorrupted mystery." St. John therefore says: "That he declared that which was from the beginning,

which he himself had seen and heard;" that is,
that he taught the doctrine of Christ as it was
originally delivered, as he had heard it from
Christ's own mouth, whose person he had seen
and felt; and that he made no additions of his
own, but only reported as a faithful witness. In
like manner he appeals, 1 John 2:13, 14, to the
elder Christians, whom he calls fathers, "because
they knew him who was from the beginning;"
that is, because they knew how Christ had taught
from the beginning; and 1 John 2:24, he says:
"Let that abide in you which ye have heard
from the beginning." Farther he says, 1 John
2:7: "Brethren, I write no new commandment
unto you, but an old commandment, which
ye had from the beginning." In the next verse,
he adds: "Again a new commandment I write
unto you, which thing is true in him and in
you, because the darkness is past, and the light
now shineth." Now Christ himself had given his
disciples a commandment, which he called a new
commandment, and this was "that they should
love one another.' The term *new commandment*,
therefore, St. John borrowed from Christ; but in
the present instance he appears to have applied
it to a different subject, because the special
command which Christ gave to his disciples, that
they should love one another, and which he called
a new commandment, could not well be called an
old commandment, being very different from the
general commandment, that we should love our
neighbor. St. John, therefore, very probably meant
that the commandment of love and sanctification
was no new commandment, as the Gnostics
contended, but the old commandment which
the Christians had heard from the beginning. It

was, indeed, become a new commandment, in consequence of the false doctrines which then prevailed; or rather, it appeared to be so, because the Gnostics had endeavored to banish it from their system of theology. But whether a new or an old commandment, St. John thought proper to enforce it. (55)

It pains me greatly to see the effect much of the media has had on trust. They have succeeded in isolating many of us by convincing us that evil is just beyond our sight or just around the corner. In my opinion, they have made us suspicious of others by portraying them as our opponent or someone to fear. Some are even teaching the listening world that Christianity is an evil effort to replace the truth of God with superstition and fear.

The world of darkness is a world of fear. Even though the chance of a kidnapping or a crime is very small we allow fear mongers to implant fear in our children and in their parents compared to the damage caused by the fear that divides us and makes us victims of another kind of danger, that of isolation. Divide and conquer is still a good strategy for any enemy and it is working in some areas of society in America today.

Superstition lives in a world of darkness and fear. One prime example of the results of superstition can be found in 1 Samuel 28:4–20: Balaam might, at one time, have been a great prophet, but because of greed and superstition, he was killed with those who participated in his superstition and destruction

The Matthew Henry Commentary tells us, "The learned bishop Patrick inclines to think, with many Jewish writers, that Balaam had been a great prophet, who, for the accomplishments of his predictions and the answers of his prayers, both for good and evil, had been looked upon justly as a man of great interest with God, but that growing proud and covetous, God departed from him, and then, to support his sinking credit, he betook himself to diabolical arts." (56)

The record of the end of Balaam and the consequences of his failure to remain loyal to God and his consequences are pointed out in scripture soon after his association with the king, Moab: "And they warred against the Midianites, as the Lord commanded Moses; and they slew all the males. They slew the kings of Midian, beside the rest of them that were slain; namely, Evi, and Rekem, and Zur, and Hur, and Reba, five kings of Midian: Balaam also the son of Beor they slew with the sword." (57)

Superstition has no place in the life of a Christian, but rather points out a lack of faith and the presence of spiritual darkness in the individual thereby causing the message of salvation to be diminished and replaced with an attitude of excessive tolerance.

Christians should be intolerant. We should be intolerant of sin and deceit. We should be intolerant of those who teach that all religion is the same, and we should be intolerant of ignorance and superstition that engenders fear in the heart of the one who believes it. It is the responsibility of every Christian to be light to those who walk in darkness to point them to a saving knowledge of the true and living God; that means we must be trusting and trustworthy in this world of insecurity, distrust, and superstition.

Because of Fear and Superstition, the World of Darkness Is a World of Insecurity

While attending a psychology class, many years ago, at Fort Rucker Alabama, I heard a captain who had been stationed in the Middle East give us this supposed Egyptian proverb. "One should trust his neighbor but tie his camel." I don't know if that is really an Egyptian proverb or not, but it certainly addresses the difference between an individual who is willing to trust those around him or not.

Because of their own untrustworthiness, the leaders of the Jews could not trust Jesus. Because of his insecurity, Abram listened to Sarah and accepted a substitute wife. Genesis 16:1–4, "Insecurity caused the man with one talent to hide it in the ground. And the one also who had received the one talent came up and said, 'Master, I knew you to be a hard man, reaping where you did not sow, and gathering where you scattered no seed and I was afraid, and went away and hid your talent in the ground; see, you have what is yours.'"(58)

The world of darkness is a world of misplaced love: There is love for the world.

My family spent a large portion of our time while we were stationed at Fort Hood Texas, witnessing to a seventeen-year-old girl. She eventually started going to church with us and became aware of some changes she needed to make in her life. When she found this out, she stopped coming, saying, "I just can't live that kind of life." (59)

Like Eve in the Garden of Eden, her love for the world and worldly living kept her out of the world of light. "Her emphasis was on herself and things that could give her pleasure. That self-centeredness is prevalent throughout the world of darkness."

The Holy Bible records of the temptation of Eve. The picture of her life is very much like the lifestyle of most of us today: "When the woman saw that the tree was good for food, and that it was a delight to the eyes, and that the tree was desirable to make one wise, she took from its fruit and ate." (60)

Later we will discuss this scripture in greater detail, but it will suffice here to say there are many evil attractions in the world.

The evil seed within us is always drawn to those evil attractions. Like a magnet, they pull us away from God into the world of darkness. 1 John 2:15 very clearly advises us to "Love not the world."

There is a love for worldly possessions. In this world where "Material is me," there is a badge of success achieved by the amount or number of possessions owned by an individual or family or group. Great wealth represents great success to them, but those who have fallen to materialistic measurement are either ignorant of or have forgotten or ignored the parable Jesus told of the man who decided to enlarge his holdings after a good crop: "Then he said, this is what I'll do: I will tear down my barns and build bigger ones, and there I will store all my grain and my goods, and I will say to myself, 'You have plenty of good things laid up for many years. Take life easy; eat drink and be merry.' But God said to him, 'You fool! This very night your life will be demanded from you, then who will get what you have prepared for yourself?'" (61)

There is an apparent love of self. Love of the world, love of possession, love of position all can be summarized in the basic term: love of self, perhaps that danger of self-worship or at least self-centeredness could be the underlying reason Christ said: "Watch out! Be on guard against all kinds of greed; a man's life does not consist in the abundance of things" (Luke 12:15).

I have heard Christians, including preachers, quote Jesus's recitation of an Old Testament phrase, "You shall love your neighbor as yourself," (Matthew 22:39) several times to claim God expects us to love ourselves.

The danger of that assertion is that often some wind up loving self too much; consequently; they become idol worshippers. They place their self on a pedestal above God. Jesus makes our position and our responsibility before God very clear: "Love the Lord your God with all your heart, and with all your mind" (Matthew 22:37).

Inordinate or excessive love of self excludes the humility and subsequent repentance necessary to be lead to the saving light that is Jesus Christ. Jesus makes the consequences of excessive love of self very clear: "I tell you the truth, unless you change and become like little children, you will never enter the kingdom of heaven" (Matthew 18:3). The apostle Paul implies the need for humility when advises those who are in the church in Rome, "Do not think of yourself more highly than you ought, but rather think of yourselves with sober judgment, in accordance with the measure of faith God has given you" (Romans 12:3).

Know who you are. Know who God is. Then look at the comparison. Then follow the advice of James, "Humble yourself before the Lord and he will lift you up" (James 4:10).

The apostle Paul puts it this way in his letter to the Philippians: "Do nothing out of selfish ambition or vain conceit, but in humility, consider others better than yourselves" (Philippians 2:3).

In my opinion, the perfect example of self-perspective can be found in the publican who put his chin to his chest and prayed, "Be merciful to me a sinner." That's the ticket to salvation. Salvation can only be accomplished through unconditional surrender. Jesus clearly advised those who would be his disciples: "If anyone would come after me, he must deny himself and take up his cross and follow me" (Matthew 16:24). Have you done that? Who is the center of your life? Can others see Jesus in you?

CHAPTER 4

Light on the Path of Righteousness Reveals What Sin Is

1 John 1:10–2:2

At a pastor's conference one Monday morning, one of my fellow pastors asked me how the previous Sunday services had gone. Before I could answer, another pastor who had visited our church that Sunday muttered disapprovingly, "He preached on sin."

He was guilty of ignoring the terrible consequences of sin. Harold C. Gardiner makes this observation in *The Treasury of Religious Spiritual Quotations*, "The greatest of all sins is the philosophizing of sin out of existence."(62)

That pastor responded correctly, even if a little too quickly. I had used a text found in 1 John 1:10–2:1–2. That text certainly is about sin. 1 John 1:10 points out, "If we claim we have not sinned, we make him (God) out to be a liar and his word has no place in our lives." But if you look beyond the title, it also includes the answer to it.

In many VBS opening assemblies, I hear the question asked, "What is sin?" Almost every time it is asked, it is described as "not being good" or "doing things that are wrong or bad." There is some merit to that answer. Ecclesiastes 7:20 points out: "Indeed there is not a righteous man on earth who continually does good and who never sins," but it is the accepted answer many times by Sunday school teachers, pastors, and VBS directors because it is a simple answer and they seem to think the children won't be able to understand the biblical description. There is more than adequate evidence; however, of the necessity for the biblical definition of sin to be presented to every extent possible or be responsible for many lost church members who believe if they just live right, everything will be all right. As many as possible must be convinced that: "All have sinned and fall short of the glory of God" (Romans 3:23). This is an attempt to explain that and the way to overcome it.

John teaches that sin is "lawlessness." It is also noted as transgression, depravity, and disruption of a right relationship with God. There are other descriptions of sin not included here. In consideration of this explanation, it becomes quite apparent that consideration of the seriousness of sin demands that it be discussed.

Sin Is an Evil Tendency.

In his book, *New Testament Theology: Thematic Study*, Donald Guthrie provides an extensive in depth discussion spanning several pages concerning the subject of sin. Included in that discussion, he describes sin as an evil tendency. He says, "Sin is an evil tendency which existed in man at the very beginning." (63)

Even the apostle Paul had trouble resisting sinful behavior. He made this confession, "So I find this law at work, when I want to do good, evil is right there with me" (Romans 7:21).

It would be impossible to count the number of men and women, both young and old, who have gone to a foreign country to serve in military service or some other occupation without family and found themselves lured into the evil of adultery or excessive drinking or some other sort of sin. Seemingly, in many cases, regardless of how hard they tried, they were unable to resist. I have personally seen many young soldiers who made the same mistake Eve made in the Garden of Eden. When Satan spoke to her in Genesis 3:1–7, she already was in trouble, she had taken her attention off her husband,

and then she took her attention off God and began to wander, consequently, when Satan spoke to her she was a willing listener to his tempting words.

Almost all those who have found themselves in the bars or homes of prostitutes were individuals who wandered out of fellowship with God and family.

Many years ago, when I was still a child, my mother and father left us with one of our cousins for a while. One of the things he taught us was a little song: "I dreamed I was goin' to heaven, ridin' on a bale of hay. I got off on the wrong road and I heard old Satan say, "Just come on in, I've got a special place picked out for you." (64)

He might have a special place picked out for you also. He beckons constantly to me and that could be the case where you're concerned, because we all have a tendency to sin.

Sin is missing the mark. Beginning on page 187 of his book pertaining to Christian theology, Donald Guthrie says, "The general form of sin (hamartia) occurs several times in the synoptic gospels, most often in the confession of sins (Mt 3:6; Mk. 1:5) or forgiveness of sins (twenty one times). Its basic meaning is failure to hit the mark." (65)

In *Baker's Dictionary of Theology*, we find a similar statement that reinforces the one made by Donald Guthrie. There he says, "While the details of the exegesis of Romans 5:12–21 are disputed, it appears certain that Paul regards all men as sinners in Adam. Not only did Adam introduce sin into the world, the fact is that death exists even where there is no mosaic law and no imputation of sin in connection with that law, therefore death must stem from the fact that, "through one trespass the judgment came unto all men to condemnation." (66)

CHAPTER 5

Light on the Path of Righteousness Reveals that Sin Has Certain Characteristics

Sin has an inherited existence. If one were to live a perfect life, he or she would still be guilty of sin because sin has an inherited existence. The Psalmist says: "Surely I was sinful at birth, sinful from the time my mother conceived me" (Psalm 51:5).

The apostle Paul explains it this way: "Therefore, just as sin entered the world—through one man, and death through sin, and in this way death came to all men" (Romans 6:12). I guess you could call it spiritually genetic predisposition. But probably not. Probably, the best way to say it is, since Adam is the beginning of the human race, his sinful nature is inherited by all his descendants—that's us.

The preceding verses support the statement of Dr. Guthrie that "sin is an evil tendency that has been in existence from the very beginning (67) as well as the statement made in *Baker's Theological Dictionary*, which point out Adam as the beginning of sin. (68)

Think about some of the behaviors, looks, or habits you have inherited from your mom or dad. Think about your size. If you are a certain height or build, you probably inherited it from a member of your family, usually mom or dad. Or perhaps the color of your eyes, or hair, or even the shape of your nose has been inherited from someone in your family. Although many of our behaviors, mannerisms, and even dispositions are learned, inheritance of some attributes we possess must be acknowledged.

Sin has an inner drive. "Sin is a tree with a great many branches, but it has only one root, namely the inordinate love of self." (69)

For many of us, there is a battle that rages within. One way to describe that experience is that sin has an inner drive. We work so hard at trying to do the right thing and lo and behold, something in us seems to slip and we find our self-doing the wrong thing.

The writer of Proverbs makes this statement concerning evil men, "An evil man is snared by his own sin" (Proverbs 29:6). Jeremiah informs us: "The heart is deceitful above all things and beyond cure, who can understand it" (Jeremiah 17:9).

Psychology speaks of drives or emotions. I wrote a book in 1983 titled *Emotions: Controlled or Controlling*, with a subtitle *The Dog Wagging the Tail* with the purpose of pointing out many positive and negative effects emotion has on our life. (70) Although I chose not to publish the book, while doing research I caught a glimpse of the power emotions can have in one's life. This power and the danger of it certainly need to be considered here because our emotions usually are the source of many of our problems.

Often when someone does something beyond explanation, they will say something like, "I just felt like it." Satan often uses our emotions (feelings) to cause us to do or think about things that are neither healthy, right, nor rational. Then we find our self in the middle of a sinful situation.

On the other hand, our emotional attachment to a Holy God can lead us to do things that are for his glory and the good of others. That's why it is so important to realize our emotions can be directed and controlled. The power and influence of Jesus Christ in our life goes far in that direction.

In conclusion, it must be said it is Christ in us who makes us conquerors of evil.

Sin Has a Learned Behavior

As was true of many psychology students, one of my tasks while studying Behavioral Science was to train a pigeon to peck a certain spot while penned in a box used for that purpose. We used what is called behavioral management. It was consisted of rewarding the pigeon for each move or gesture he made in the direction of the spot mounted on a cardboard wheel with the result that he would eventually peck the spot on the wheel. (71)

That procedure also works on human beings. I know because I have done it, both in an institution and out. Not with a cardboard wheel of course, but with some type of positive reinforcement (reward) for desired behavior. That is really what happens when some young person, or even someone older, is rewarded with an approving smile or some other desired gesture; and more convincingly with a material reward.

Children are rewarded for deviant behavior (sin) when parents or older siblings offer verbal approval or laugh at their behavior or give them favorable attention immediately following the deed performed. Many very sinful activities are first noticed in a home, or family setting, committed by an admired individual. Have you ever heard someone tell their child not to smoke while smoking themselves? It is true, actions do speak louder than words. It is also true that much sinful behavior has been learned by watching someone else do it. That is the reference alluded to in Proverbs 22:6, "Train a child in the way he should go, and when he is old he will not depart from it."

Sin Is Concealed by Hypocrisy

Continuing in sin while pretending piety is hypocrisy. Sin reveals the lack of authenticity of a profession of faith. In every denomination, there are those who profess Christ as their Savior yet live a deplorable lifestyle.

While serving in the military service I was often compelled to go to bars for various reasons. Sometimes I went because that was the only place to get a coke or some other soft drink; at other times, however, I went for a more serious reason. Sometimes it was my duty to guard premises or to help remove a problem from the area. It has often been the case that someone would come up to me in a drunken stupor and attempt to tell me what kind of Christian he was.

There have been occasions where prostitutes tried to convince me they were Christians. Each time I felt it my duty to explain to them that I am not their judge. I'm not yours either, but I would like to point out one scripture for your benefit: "By their fruit you will recognize them." (Matthew 7:16). John tells us, "No one who lives in him keeps on sinning. No one who continues to sin has either seen him or known him. (1 John 3:6)

Artificially covering sin is hypocrisy; false piety is an artificial covering.

There are those who practice false piety. I heard a member of a local church speak of piety in a negative way and criticize the pious. It is my opinion he was really speaking of those who claim piety while living in the darkness of a lost world. *Baker's Dictionary of Theology* describes piety as: "Having begun with a man named P. J. Spencer who worked for a spiritual purpose through the program announced in his Pia Desideria, his emphasis being on an informal gathering for prayer, Bible study, and the nurture of the Christian life within the framework of orthodox doctrine and allegiance." (72) That sounds much like a thing sorely needed today.

If *Baker's Dictionary of Theology* describes piety as noted above, perhaps it is time to consider those who act as if they are indeed pious while seeking rewards for themselves by that behavior as possessing false piety.

Religious people, including those who have been baptized and possibly even joined a church, can be beautiful on the outside but hollow or even rotten on the inside.

In the recent past we had a beautiful maple tree in our backyard. Its branches covered much of the yard. It was too big to reach around with your arms. What a magnificent sight. One day a storm came. The wind split that beautiful tree in half. We were amazed! It was mostly hollow and rotted away.

The Pharisees of Jesus's day were like that. Jesus called them whited sepulchers, or graves, He described them in these words, "Woe unto you teachers of the law and Pharisees; you hypocrites!

You are like whitewashed tombs, which look beautiful on the outside, but on the inside are full of dead men's bones." (73)

True conversion, authentic Christian experience, is a matter of the heart. Salvation is a change of heart, a change of mind, and a change of behavior. Clipping the branches from a tree only changes the shape of the tree; true salvation is changing the roots. Salvation is creation of a new creature. Paul makes that clear when he says: "Therefore, if anyone is in Christ, he is a new creation; the old has gone, the new has come" (2 Corinthians 5:17). Eventually, evidence of pretense will be revealed, either in this time or on judgment day.

False piety is as sinful as any obvious sin committed, eventually it too will be revealed by behavior. Probably one of the most disappointing experiences of my ministry has been those who have made a profession of their faith, were baptized and continued to walk in sin. Conversion means change. If there has been no change, there has been no conversion. Jesus made that very clear when he informed his audience: "Verily I say unto you, except ye become converted, and become as little children, ye shall not enter into the kingdom of heaven" (Matthew 18:3 KJV). It is stated differently in the NIV, but the meaning is the same: "I tell you the truth, unless you change and become like children, you will never enter the kingdom of heaven."

Church membership can be an artificial cover. Churches spend a large amount of time attempting to get straying church members back in church. Books have been written about it, including one titled *Reclaiming Inactive Church Members.* (74)

Much of that time and effort should be spent trying to bring them to an authentic experience in Christ. Scripture makes it very clear: "No one who lives in him keeps on sinning, No one who continues to sin has either seen him or known him" (1 John 3:6).

I was once tricked into baptizing a young man who was living in adultery. He introduced the woman with whom he was living as his wife. Although I had visited with him several times and counseled with him, He never told me about his adulterous behavior, nor did the church, though some of them knew about it. After I found out, I worked diligently to show him scriptures pointing out his situation. Nothing worked. When I left, he was still claiming to be a Christian and living in adultery. I believe the Bible is the inerrant infallible word of God. I believe when it says in Revelations 21:8, "Adulterers cannot enter the kingdom of God." That's what it means. (75)

I have personally witnessed to individuals who were living deep in sin who had "joined the church" sometime in the distant past. Some could even remember the date. Most of them, when asked if they plan to go to heaven when they die, have answered yes, yet there is no evidence of authentic conversion. You might say, "They don't have to prove their conversion to you." I'll give you that when you start getting tomatoes from a peach tree.

Many preachers and teachers have made the point, "If you were not converted when you joined the church and was baptized, you just got a free bath." But it really wasn't free. "The wages of sin is death" (Romans 6:23). To me, that means someday all who are pretend Christians will pay for their sins. I'm not qualified to judge, but God is.

The Psalmist declares: "You know when I sit and when I rise; you perceive my thoughts from afar, you discern my going out and my lying down; you are familiar with all my ways" (Psalms 139:2–4)

We are informed that sinner and saint will grow together until the day of harvest in a parable from Jesus: "Let both grow together until the harvest. At that time, I will tell the harvesters: 'First collect the weeds and tie them into bundles to be burned; then gather the wheat and bring it into the barn'"

How about you? Have you been converted or are you one of those who are beautiful on the outside but rotten on the inside? Or maybe you joined some church somewhere and thought that was enough. Let's look at 1 John 3:6 again. "No one who lives in him keeps on sinning. No one who continues to sin has either seen him or known him."

CHAPTER 6

Light on the Path of Righteousness Reveals What Sin Does

1 John 1:6, 8, 10

After you have heard someone tell a lie, do you believe him when he tells you he's not lying the next time he tells you something? Why not? Could it be because his credibility has been weakened by the sin of lying to you? This is exactly the sin pointed out in 1John. He makes it very clear that claiming to be a Christian is a lie unless you have had a personal encounter with Jesus Christ. He informs us that, "If we claim to have fellowship with him yet walk in darkness, we lie and do not the truth" (1 John1:6).

One perspective concerning those who practice sin is that sin is as much an indicator as a determinate. J. Vernon McGee rightly points out eternal security of the believer in his discussion concerning the advocacy of Christ in chapter two, (76) but is it possible that John is making the point here that not everyone in the church is in Christ?

A reminder of the consequences of sin is very important today. Because, in many cases, our children are taught it is better to lie than hurt someone's feelings or to get what you want or when theft is practiced as a matter of course and considered normal in some social circles it is time to point out to children and parents alike that lies can keep us out of the kingdom of God.

The Bible teaches very plainly that sin has consequences. John points this out when he says: "But the cowardly, the unbelieving, the vile, the murderers, the sexually immoral, those who practice magic arts, the idolaters, and all liars—their place will be in the fiery lake of sulfur. This is the second death." (77)

Sin does many bad and despicable things to its victims or perpetrators or both, none of them good; many of them horrific.

Sin degenerates and degrades. The Preacher's Homiletic Commentary puts it this way, "It is among the most potent of energies of sin, that it leads astray by blinding and blinds by leading astray." (78)

Great men and women have been destroyed because of their yielding one time to the temptation of sin. It is not possible to discuss all the ramifications and implications that come to mind with this word *sin*. But according to the Preacher's Homiletic Commentary, "A man in sympathy with darkness cannot be in fellowship with light." (79)

Sin separates us from God. The *Holman Bible Handbook* tells us, "The disobedience of Adam and Eve alienated them from God and each other." (8)

"So the Lord banished him from the Garden of Eden to work the ground from which he had been taken. After he drove the man out, he placed on the east side of the Garden of Eden cherubim and a flaming sword flashing back and forth to guard the way to the tree of life." (81)

Notice the word *claim* in 1 John 1:6 NIV: "If we claim to have fellowship with him yet walk in darkness, we lie and do not the truth."

This was a struggle for me because, as with others who have studied this text, I ascertained it was written to Christians. It was written to a church. Although, in a perfect church everyone would be a Christian, churches aren't perfect; therefore, here is a message to the church member who claims to be a Christian "claims to have fellowship with God" but does not. John says this person lies and does not the truth.

Matthew Henry puts it this way: "This conclusion issues into two branches: for the conviction of such professors who have no fellowship . . . They belie God; for he holds no heavenly fellowship or intercourse with unholy souls." (82)

That fits in with the words of Jesus in John 10:27: "My sheep listen to my voice; I know them and they follow me."

A story I heard one time sort of makes it more clear.

Alexander the Great was sitting on a disciplinary hearing one day when a young man came in. "What is your name?" Alexander the Great asked the young man.

"Alexander, sir," was the reply.

"Change your ways or change your name" was the response from Alexander the Great. (83)

Maybe that would be good advice for those who claim they walk in fellowship with God but live a life to please the world.

James offers a word to those who claim to have fellowship with God and walk in darkness: "You, adulterous people, don't you know that friendship with the world is hatred toward God? Anyone who chooses to be a friend of the world becomes an enemy of God" (James 4:4).

Continuing Matthew Henry's point on verse six: "For the conviction and consequent satisfaction of those who are near to God: but if we walk in the light as He is in the light, we have fellowship one with another, and the blood of Jesus Christ cleanses us from all sin." (84)

Here, in 1 John 2:1, is found the one who is walking in the light but stumbles from time to time. This is the description of one who has fellowship with God. Who, when he stumbles, is convicted and repents. These are the people John calls "my little children."

The Beacon Bible Commentary says: "A man who chooses the sphere of darkness in which to live does not know fellowship with God and with his children." (85)

According to Adam Clarke's Commentary, having fellowship, communion, with God, necessarily implies partaking of the divine nature: "Now, if a man profess to have such communion, and walk in darkness—live an irreligious and sinful life, he lies, in the profession which he makes." (86)

Sin separates some from others. Prisons are just about everywhere to confirm the fact that sin separates some from others. There is probably a myriad of reasons for this. I am going to list a few of the basic ones for us to consider.

Sin separates between good and bad. Our prisons exist for the separation of bad people from good people. They're probably not the best solution and certainly not the only solution, but they do accomplish protection for those who can't always protect themselves.

There are other ways sin causes individuals to be separated from society. Sometimes they are just shunned or pushed aside because of distrust or disgust; or perhaps even because of fear. When enough people have enough fear of an individual, they will find a way to isolate him.

There is another way sin separates; that is because of social preference. Most of my life I have heard, "Birds of a feather, flock together." I took that to mean bad people usually like to hang around with other bad people. I don't know if that is because of rejection by society as a whole, but I suspect a case could be made for that point of view. On the other hand, many who commit sin isolate themselves because they prefer secrecy, or because of their distrust of others or to avoid the pain inflicted on them by the rest of society.

Our behavior is predominantly a mirror of our heart. Someone has said, "Where the heart goes, the heels will soon follow." It is my observation that that statement is borne out time and time again. That's why it is so important to understand that salvation must be a change of heart, a change of mind, and a change of behavior.

Sin brings confusion. The sin of Achan in Joshua, chapter seven, caused the spies to be confused about the number of those who dwelt at Ai. Joshua 7:3: "When they returned to Joshua, they said, 'Not all the people need to go up against Ai. Send two or three thousand men to take it and do not weary all the people, for only a few men are there." Joshua 8:25: "Twelve thousand men and women fell that day—all the people of Ai." Is it possible that God confused the spies because of sin in their camp? The Preacher's Homiletic Commentary puts forth this speculation: "God was not with the spies to enlighten them, and therefore they were deceived." (87)

When I was a lad of seventeen, I decided to go out on my own, as they say, in my part of the country. I went to Wichita, Kansas. It wasn't long before I decided I could get along without God and family. Eventually I found work at an airplane factory and fell in with a couple of men who worked there. They took me to the home of one of them where they introduced me to an "exotic drink." I have regretted that night ever since it happened. I had gotten away from family. I had gotten away from God and became confused about right and wrong and paid a terrible price for the confusion in my life caused by sin. (88)

Sin causes weakness. "So about three thousand men went up, but they were routed by the men of Ai" (Joshua 7:4). It is possible that much of the weakness experienced by the Israelites before Ai was initiated by shame and confusion.

It is certainly plausible that everyone in Achan's family knew what had been done; possibly others could have known or suspected also. That would cause them to share the confusion and shame of Achan.

One thing is sure—when an individual has committed a sin as grievous as that of Achan, it will affect their attitude and behavior unless it has been an established pattern, in which case it will be known or suspected by others anyway.

On the other hand, the weakness they experienced could have been instituted by God himself. He does have that capability, you know, and I believe a personal God is able, and does, bring hardship into our life as a form of discipline. The writer of Hebrews gives this advice: "My son, do not make light of the Lord's discipline, and do not lose heart when he rebukes you, because the Lord disciplines those he loves and punishes everyone he accepts as a son."

Sin brings fear. Because of the defeat at the hands of the citizens of Ai, it is reported: "At this the hearts of the people melted" (Joshua 7:5b). Preacher's Homiletic Commentary informs us that, "All defeat does not bring fear. Sometimes it stimulates. But when men are forced to face failure for their transgressions against God, fear is a certain result." (88)

There is a fear of discovery. Achan hid his loot in the ground inside his tent. There are as many different and devious ways to hide sin as there are sinners. Some attempt to cover it and pretend nothing is wrong, such as those in 1 John 1:6 who walk in darkness but claim fellowship with God.

Some representatives of the faith claim our churches contain an unbelievable number of members who claim to be Christians but have never had a personal encounter with Jesus Christ. That pretense works with those around us. But God looked in the tent of Achan. He saw the object hidden under the dirt. He saw into Achan's heart and knew there was sin in the camp. Someone had disobeyed his instructions.

The fear of discovery could be coupled with another fear Although it is not always the case, there is the fear of consequences to be considered

Today there is a sort of trend to deny fear of God. Some call it "being in awe," but the Bible teaches, in Proverbs 1:7, "Fear of the Lord is the beginning of knowledge, but fools despise wisdom and discipline."

It would take very little imagination to picture what was going through the mind of Achan as Joshua systematically worked his way through the congregation until it was narrowed down to his family. It is totally plausible to believe Achan knew the consequences of his sin and was looking forward to it with great trepidation; even in the Old Testament, the wages of sin was death.

Although death is the ultimate consequence of sin, it produces many other consequences, some we have discussed previously and in the following paragraph we have added a few more.

Sin brings suffering and sorrow. The suffering and sorrow experienced by Joshua are reported this way: "Then Joshua tore his clothes and fell face down to the ground before the ark of the Lord, remaining there till evening. The elders of Israel did the same and sprinkled dust on their heads" (Joshua 7:6).

When Adam and Eve were disobedient before God, He informed them of the suffering they had brought upon themselves: "To the woman he said, 'I will greatly increase your pains in childbearing; with pain, you will give birth to your children.'"

To Adam he said, "Because you listened to your wife and ate from the tree about which I commanded you, 'you must not eat of it,' cursed is the ground because of you; through painful toil you will eat of it all the days of your life" (89).

One has but to look around or read a newspaper or watch TV or listen to a radio to realize the suffering caused by sin: The loss of life, the loss of freedom, the loss of safety, are everywhere we look.

Since prayer has been taken out of public places to a very great extent, and Christianity has begun to be treated by the media as "Just another religion," and as the Ten Commandments have been removed, we have watched morality decline in America. As morality and lawfulness decline crime, suffering, and sorrow climb because sin is lawlessness and it is exemplified by those who have turned from lawful and moral living to the sin of self-worship.

The end product of sin is everlasting death. In the book of Romans, it is pointed out by the apostle Paul, "The wages of sin is death, but the gift of God is everlasting life through Jesus Christ our Lord" (Romans 6:23).

If it is true that, "All have sinned and fall short of the glory of God" (Romans 3:23), and there is abundant verification of that possibility when we consider that there are at last three ways sin is a part of our existence how can anyone escape?

Sin is not new. It has always been, that's the reason we should grasp the full extent and meaning of the word sin.

It is important to understand that sin and its consequence of everlasting death have been in existence from Adam until now. The apostle Paul points out this reality when writing to the Romans: "Nevertheless, death reigned from Adam to Moses, even over those who had not sinned according to the likeness of the transgression of Adam, who is a type of him who is to come." (90)

Inherited sin is different than sins of commission or the sin of omission; it is a much deeper type of sin.

Paul described this type of sin this way in Ephesians: "All of us also lived among them at one time, gratifying the cravings of our sinful nature and following its desires and thoughts" (Ephesians 2:3).

Throughout the Bible, you see "this sinful nature" referred to in different ways and different forms as the basic cause or drive for sin.

The same verse explains the destiny of those who are recipients of the sinful nature. "Like the rest," Paul says, "we were by nature objects of wrath," (Ephesians 2:3). That wrath is described in other places as everlasting death. The Revelation of John describes it most vividly: "And I saw the dead both great and small standing before the throne, and books were opened. Another book was opened, which is the book of life. The dead were judged according to what they had done as recorded in the books. The sea gave up the dead that were in it, and death and Hades gave up the dead that were in them, and each person was judged according to what he had done. Then death and Hades were thrown into the lake of fire. The lake of fire is the second death. If anyone's name was not found in the Book of Life, he was thrown into the lake of fire." (91)

CHAPTER 7

Light on the Path of Righteousness Reveals the Solution for Sin

1 John 1:8, 10; 2:1

The solution for sin begins with understanding conviction. A pastor in Alabama told me a story of another preacher who had preached a sermon he thought he had been lead to preach. After the service was over, he went to visit with the congregation. As he walked out into the yard, one of those attending that service hit him and knocked him down. Apparently, something he had said caused the listener to be angry (or convicted). (92)

When God touches our heart, convicts us of sin, and calls us to salvation, reaction can vary drastically. One example is Samuel who thought at first Eli was calling him:

> One night Eli, whose eyes were becoming so weak that he could barely see, was lying down in his usual place. The lamp of God had not yet gone out, and Samuel was lying down in the temple of the Lord where the ark of God was, then the Lord called Samuel.
>
> Samuel answered, "Here I am," and he ran to Eli and said, "Here I am; you called me." But

Eli said, "I did not call; go back and lay down."
So he went and lay down.

Again, the Lord called, "Samuel," and
Samuel got up and went to Eli and said, "Here I
am, you called me."

Now Samuel did not yet know the Lord.
The word of the Lord had not yet been revealed
to him.

The Lord called Samuel the third time, and
Samuel got up and went to Eli and said, "Here
I am; you called me." Then Eli realized that the
Lord was calling the boy so Eli told Samuel, "Go
and lie down, and if he calls you say, 'Speak for
your servant is listening.'" So Samuel went and
lay down in his place. The Lord came and stood
there calling as at other times, "Samuel! Samuel!"
Then Samuel said "Speak for your servant is
listening." (94)

This is a story of a young preacher who explained his calling
this way during his sermon: "One day, I was out in the field plowing
and decided to take a break. While looking up at the clouds I saw the
letters G. P. I understood them to mean, go preach'. As the congregation filed out the door after the service, one of the deacons shook
the young preacher's hand and said, 'Did you ever think it could have
meant go plow?'" (94)

I'm sure, on a serious note, there have been those who were
uncomfortable after hearing a message from God but didn't understand what it was about or disliked the application.

We have already spoken about Isaiah and the Apostle Paul in
their experiences as they dealt with conviction in their life and a few
others as examples. It is my prayer that this effort might open the
spiritual eyes of an individual to whom God is speaking even now.

Conviction begins with the realization of the difference between
good and evil. John's letter addresses a problem created by a group
called Gnostics. J. Vernon McGee calls them the "real enemies of

Christianity." He says in his book on 1 John, "Gnosticism was the real enemy of Christianity, and, my friend, it still is." (95)

The Apostle Paul makes this point: "All who sin apart from the law will also perish apart from the law, and all who sin will be judged by the law" (Romans 2:12).

Does that mean one must study and learn the laws of every land? No. He makes it clear that:

> Indeed, when Gentiles, who do not have the law do by nature things required by the law, they are a law for themselves even though they do not have the law, since they show that the requirements of the law are written on their hearts, their consciences also bearing witness, and their thoughts now accusing them, now defending them. (96)

This scripture points out that everyone who is responsible for making decisions about life has, the ability to know right from wrong.

Although Paul speaks often of the law and individual responsibility, he repeatedly informs us that the law does not save but that it is a guide to point individuals to the saving grace of Jesus Christ. He says, "Clearly no one is justified before God by the law" (Galatians 3:11).

In another place, he points out: "The righteous will live by faith."

He makes it very clear that there is a different mind-set between those who are saved and those who are not when he informs us that, "The mind of sinful man is death but the mind controlled by the Spirit is life and peace" (Romans 8:6).

John McArthur informs us that the Gnostics of whom John was writing had three levels of denial: "They ignored their sin as if it were not a reality to them; they claimed to have no sin then, perhaps with some pride, claimed they had never sinned. They justified this claim in their own minds because they maintained a belief that the body and spirit were separate entities." (97)

J. Vernon McGee states, "This belief had one primary principle which basically stated was: "Matter, or material, was essentially evil; only the spirit was good." (98)

Conviction comes with realization of the consequences of sin: "The soul who sins is the one who will die" (Ezekiel 18:4b).

There is a death described in the Bible that goes far beyond the death we will experience after we spend a few years here on earth. It is the everlasting destination of all who refuse Jesus Christ as Savior. Because of the gravity and the seriousness of this consequence I must repeat it here: the book of Revelation spells it out very graphically: "And I saw the dead, great and small. Standing before the throne, and books were opened, and another book was opened which is the book of life. The dead were judged according to what they had done as recorded in the books. Then death and Hades were thrown into the lake of fire. The lake of fire is the second death." (99)

One of the reasons everlasting death is considered everlasting destruction is made clear a little later when John reveals: "If anyone's name was not found written in the book of life, he was thrown into the lake of fire" Revelation 20:15.

The apostle Paul offers more information concerning everlasting destruction: "He will punish those who do not know God and do not obey the gospel of our Lord Jesus. They will be punished with everlasting destruction and shut out of the presence of the Lord and from the majesty of his power." (100)

Conviction brings realization and consideration of the promises of God. Since all have sinned and fall short of the glory of God and since the everlasting punishment for sin is so severe, who could face it without some trepidation; especially if there were no alternative or escape. But God has promised all those who will come to him everlasting life. Jesus said, "Most assuredly, I say to you, he who believes in me has everlasting life" (John 6:47).

Isaiah offers his invitation with that same promise: "Come now, let us reason together, says the Lord; though your sins be as scarlet, they shall be white as snow, though they be red as crimson, they shall be like wool" (Isaiah 1:18).

Included in the promise of everlasting life are many other promises Christians can consider as we work through the struggles and the victories in this world. Peter described them in his second letter to those who had been scattered (dispersed).

Peter gives those who had been scattered an insight and a reason for encouragement and in doing so to all those who have authentically accepted Christ Jesus as Lord and Savior. He informed us that: "His (God's) divine power has given us everything we need for life and godliness through our knowledge of him who called us by his own glory and goodness. Through these he has given us very great and precious promises so that through them you may participate in the divine nature and escape the corruption in the world caused by evil desires." (101)

We are all looking forward to that day when Jesus comes to take us home, and what a day that will be. But there is a twofold connotation in the promise Peter just pointed out that there is certainly a promise for that glorious day, but there is also a promise for now: "His divine power has given us everything we need for life" Paul supports this when he says, "We know that in all things God works for the good of those who love him" (Romans 8:28).

Conviction Comes with Personal Application

Dr. Dubois, president of the Baptist Bible Institute in Graceville, Florida, made this observation: "One of the reasons many people miss out on the gospel is because they are too busy sharing it. They share it with the person in front of them and the one behind them and the one on either side, then, there is nothing left for them." (102)

I'm not sure how often this is true but I can see where it does apply in some cases.

David attempted to blame others when Nathan, the prophet, came to admonish him concerning his sordid performance with Bathsheba and the killing of her husband, Uriah. The story told by Nathan begins by telling David: "Now a traveler came to the rich man, but the rich man refrained from taking one of his own sheep or cattle to prepare a meal for the traveler who had come to him. Instead, he took a ewe lamb that belonged to a poor man and prepared it for the one who had come to him." The Bible tells us, "David burned with anger against the man and said to Nathan, 'As surely as the Lord lives, the man who did this deserves to die! He must pay for that lamb four times over, because he who did such a thing had no pity.' Then Nathan said, 'You are the man!'" (104)

Conviction of Our Own Sinfulness and Need for a Savior Comes from Personal Application

Paul made conviction personal when he told the Ephesians: "And you he made alive, who were dead in transgressions and sins" (Ephesians 2:1 NKJV).

In verse four of that same chapter he makes salvation a personal act of God's grace: "But because of his great love for us, God, who is rich in mercy made us alive in Christ even when we were dead in transgressions."

In a Bible study course taken some years ago, the textbook written by Wally Metz points out the personal application found in Ephesians. He writes: "Two persons are in view in verse one of Ephesians, chapter 2: *you* and *he*. The *you* describes someone who is dead and who needed to be 'quickened.' The *he* describes the only one who has been raised from the dead that can do that—God."

A dead man cannot bring himself to life, it has to be someone else. That is why man is totally dependent upon God for salvation." (104)

Notice the personal nature of the sermon Peter preached on the day of Pentecost. The Holy Spirit touched and convicted each individual in a very personal way: "Now when the people heard this, they were cut to the heart" (Acts 2:37).

Did Zacchaeus have to climb a sycamore tree to be noticed by Jesus? Did Saul have to torture Christians to be noticed by Jesus? How many of us believe we must do or say something special to be noticed by Jesus? Here is his answer: "Here I am, I stand at the door and knock. If anyone hears my voice and opens the door, I will come in and eat with him and he with me" (Revelation 3:20).

Holy personal application is a vehicle of the Spirit: "When he comes, he will convict the world of guilt, in regard to sin and righteousness and judgment" (John 16:8).

As two individuals walked down the road toward Emmaus that day after the crucifixion of Christ, they were discussing the events that had just occurred and some of the rumors going around. They were confused. They didn't know if, in fact, Jesus had risen, as some had said. They didn't know what the future might hold for their own lives. How perplexed and distressed they must have been.

Jesus came to them in the depth of their confusion. Luke tells it like this, "As they talked and discussed these things with each other, Jesus himself came up and walked alongside them" (Luke 24:15).

Wow! What an experience that must have been! But it should be noted, they didn't recognize him immediately.

Then their hearts began to experience an urge for him to continue with them so he stayed and taught them the scripture pertaining to him and the biblical references concerning his crucifixion and resurrection: "And beginning with Moses and the prophets he explained to them what was said in all the scriptures concerning himself." (105)

Was their urge for his companionship initiated by the Holy Spirit of God? I believe it was because after the breaking of bread and the blessing, their eyes were opened and they recognized him. Although some might see this event as irrelevant, I see it as the Holy Spirit working with Jesus in revelation.

What makes this so great? Jesus came to them! He came to them in the depth of their confusion.

Some would tell you that conviction is a matter of conscience. That is not always true. In different geographical areas, there are different ideas and practices of morality. What's wrong in Texas might be completely different in Uganda; therefore, our conscience would not necessarily be reliable that is one more reason for an understanding of the source of sin as not only about behavior but of inheritance and nature. When the whole picture is put in perspective, it becomes apparent that the Holy Spirit works in those places and around the world.

Jesus came to them when they were confused. Not about morality, but about salvation.

The Holy Spirit created the hunger for his companionship. The desire of these two men on the road to Emmaus for the company of Jesus was not because he was a great hero on a white horse, but because he was the resurrected Jesus, the Savior of the world.

The Holy Spirit caused the "burning in their hearts" at the presence of Jesus. They asked each other, "Were not our hearts burning within us while he talked with us on the road and opened the scriptures to us?" (Luke 24:32).

The Holy Spirit opened their eyes so they could recognize Jesus at the breaking of bread, "When he was at the table with them, he took bread and gave thanks, broke it and gave it to them then their eyes were opened and they recognized him" (Luke 24:30).

Was it the way he broke the bread? No! Was it the way he prayed? No! It had to be the work of the Holy Spirit who opened their eyes. The scripture doesn't say, "They opened their eyes." It clearly says, "Their eyes were opened." Opened by whom? It had to be the Holy Spirit working in unison with Jesus at that moment.

In this great text concerning the meeting of Jesus with the men on the road to Emmaus three things are pointed out about salvation and about the solution to sin: (1) Jesus came to these individuals personally in the depth of their confusion. They had heard rumors about how his crucifixion and resurrection had affected others and they were confused. (2) They were ignorant of the pertinent scriptures. Jesus came to them personally and opened their understanding. (3) They were despondent. Jesus came and personally broke bread and opened their eyes to his presence and to a future of new possibilities.

The Emmaus road incident is only one of many incidents where Jesus took the initiative. He still takes the initiative through the avenue of the Holy Spirit.

Donald Guthrie makes it clear in his book on New Testament Theology that salvation is a spiritual experience initiated by the Holy Spirit. He points out the statement made by Jesus: "That which is born of flesh is flesh, and that which is born of spirit is spirit" (John 3:6). "The main thrust is in the fact that the new birth cannot be achieved through 'flesh', only through 'Spirit', in this case the Holy Spirit." The Father "draws" (John 6:44; cf. 6:37, 39; 17:2, 6, 9, 12, 24) but man must believe. "The statement that is borne out that. The Spirit gives life; the flesh counts for nothing" (John 6:63). That, in my view, indicates the working of the Holy Spirit in our life because the spirit of man is basically evil and prefers not to know God." (106)

Later Guthrie points out the spiritual initiative from the Father by explaining that salvation is in fact a gift from God.

"Several passages show the Spirit to be a gift from the Father (John 14:16, 26), or from the Son (15:26; 16:7), cannot be works." The initiative belongs to God. (107)

It is imperative that it is understood that salvation cannot be by works of the flesh, but by faith and faith is a matter of the Holy Spirit and is a gift from God: "For it is by grace you have been saved through faith, and that not of yourselves, it is a gift from God" (Ephesians 2:8). It is the Holy Spirit that calls us to salvation. Jesus makes that emphatically clear when he says, "No one can come to me unless the Father who sent me draws him, and I will raise him up on the last day" (John 6:44).

The Solution for Sin Is Made Complete in Christ

The original writings of the Bible were not divided by chapter or verse therefore this would be a smooth continuation pertaining to sin.

Notice those to whom the letter is addressed: "My dear children" (1 John 2:1).

These are not those individuals who: "claim to have fellowship with him yet walk in darkness" (1John 1:6). These are children who walk in the light, but stumble from time to time. J. Vernon McGee makes this remark concerning those who walk in the light: "When we walk in the light, we will see just how far we have fallen short of what God wants." (108)

Some commentators claim the possibility that these who are addressed as dear children are those who have come to Christ under the ministry of John. Others suggest his age as a reason to refer to them this way. Either is possible. Conjecture detracts from the central message here.

The difference in the dear children of verse one and those who walk in darkness is: The sincere child of God wants to please God. The Psalmist expressed it this way: "Search me, O God, and know my heart; test me and know my anxious thoughts" (Psalm 139:23–24)

"If we sin." One could say the possibility of an individual sinning is much more a foregone conclusion than a possibility. The writer of Ecclesiastes informs us: "There is not a righteous man on all the earth who does what is right and never sins" (Ecclesiastes 7:20). The good news is that: "We have an advocate with the Father" (1 John 2:1KJV). The NIV addresses it this way: "But if anybody does sin, we have one who speaks to the Father in our defense."

This advocacy is God's answer to our sinfulness. Advocacy is a legal term meaning someone who comes along side of you and helps to defend against the charges. The word advocate in the King James Version comes from the same word (*paraclete*) meaning one who comes along side of us and is translated as helper or counselor or as in John 16:7 KJV, "Comforter." The NIV simply describes the activity of an advocate.

In most cases, a lawyer, or someone trained in law, serves as our representative, if we are required to go to court for some reason. They usually have a certificate or some other means to confirm their eligibility to serve in that capacity but the best of them fall a long way short of the qualifications to represent us in the divine court of God.

Our advocate is Jesus himself. His qualifications are granted for the special purpose of pleading our case before the throne of grace. In 1 John 2:1, he is called, "Jesus Christ, the righteous one."

Jesus is qualified to be our advocate because he has been where we are. There is infinite comfort in knowing: "We have one who has been tempted in every way—just as we are—yet without sin" (Hebrews 4:15).

The temptations he endured immediately after his baptism are a small sample of all the other temptations that came to him; some we know about but I suspect there were many that remain unrecorded or not remembered. Consider the temptation to surrender as he was tortured, taunted, and hung on the cross in our place, yet he continued to complete his mission.

He is qualified to be our advocate because he is all powerful. When he stands to plead our case, he stands in all the power and glory God has given him. In Matthew 28:18 KJV, he told his disciples, "All power is given me in heaven and on earth. Can you even imagine what that's worth?"

During my ministry, I have known two young men who were convicted of killing their babies; both because of a temper fit.

As their pastor, I felt it my duty to stand by their family as much as possible. What they did was terrible. One of them kicked his little three-year-old stepdaughter in the stomach; the other one banged the head of his one year old daughter against the bedpost. I sat in the courtroom time after time with them.

I visited them, wrote letters on their behalf. Not because they were innocent but because they were more than one act of rage.

I was powerless. I couldn't erase what they had done. I couldn't plead their case for them because I had no power insofar as the court was concerned.

Their attorneys worked to get the best deal possible but they were not able to set them free. They were guilty. (109)

We are all guilty of sin in one form or another! But the good news is that Jesus has the power to set us free! We have an advocate! He is the all-powerful Jesus Christ, the righteous one. His power is without limits or restrictions.

CHAPTER 8

Spiritual Light Is Provided for Walking the Path of Righteousness

1 John 2:3–10

Walking with Christ in the biblical sense includes every sense of life. It includes intellectual, experiential, spiritual, and emotional knowledge.

Several commentators have concluded that one of the reasons John wrote his first epistle was to combat heresy within the church. *The New Commentary on The Whole Bible* says, "One of the reasons that prompted his first epistle was that a heretical faction had developed within the Church." (110)

Donald Guthrie explains in his book on New Testament Theology, "John is more concerned to warn the readers about the erroneous teaching, and to build up a positive antidote, than about the nature of the community," (which is assumed rather than stated).

Many commentaries identify a group called Gnostics with a certain amount of certainty. (111)

In my opinion, this is the heresy alluded to in 1 John 1:6 when he says, "If we claim to have fellowship with him and walk in darkness, we lie and do not live by the truth." The message found in 1 John 2:3–10 makes that point even more salient.

Walking the Christian Walk Begins with Obedience

Obedience is evidence of salvation. John makes it very clear that proof of authentic salvation is observed in those who walk the walk of obedience: "We know that we have come to know him if we obey his commands" (1 John 2:3). That walk begins with a positive response to his call to conversion and continues throughout life.

The beginning of obedience is unconditional surrender. True obedience is more than just following orders or direction. Guy H. King advances the very pertinent point in his book titled, *The Fellowship*, that it is a matter of the heart, head and lifestyle. He informs us that: "Obedience is a measure . . . If doing what He says is a test of whether we really know Him, the same token is a measure of how much we love Him. As John records in chapter 15 of his gospel, Our Lord chose a very familiar process of nature to press home the fundamental necessity of the believer to abide in Him." Jesus said in John 14:15, "If anyone loves me, he will obey my commands." (112)

True and authentic obedience is unconditional surrender. Jesus made that apparent when he told his disciples, Matthew 16:24 "If anyone would come after me, he must deny himself and take up his cross and follow me."

There is an obvious difference in the behavior of those who are in the army and those who are committed to service in the army.

In my twenty years as a soldier in the US Army, I observed individuals who were unwilling participants in military things as well as individuals who had adapted their attitude and their behavior to reflect that being a soldier was more than an occupation.

For those who considered the army a way of life and those who did not, that attitude was reflected in attitude and behavior.

Many of those who have retired or had gotten out for some other reason beyond their control, still maintain the attitude and mannerisms of a soldier. To some, these individuals could be considered fanatics.

You possibly know someone you consider a fanatical Christian. Allow me to ask if you are a sports fan. Perhaps you are a fan of football or basketball? The word fan is an abbreviation of the word fanatic. I have known people who lived and breathed sports, sort of. They could tell you yardage, interceptions, touchdowns, RBIs, strikeouts—even the size and weight of the players—but you seldom heard them talk about Jesus. I'm sorry to say some of those individuals called themselves pastors and preachers.

Yes! I'm a Jesus fan. I know very little about sports. I was not very good at any of them growing up because of poverty and inconvenience, but I am a Jesus fan. I surrendered to Jesus many years ago, while I was still a little boy. That doesn't mean I haven't strayed or brought shame to his precious name. I have. But in my insufficient and haphazard way I have surrendered to him.

My Bible teaches that salvation is unconditional surrender. Have you surrendered yourself to Jesus? Can others see Jesus in you? If they can't, maybe he really isn't there.

Genuine obedience involves genuine conversion. Conversion means change. Jesus said in John 3:3 "I tell you the truth no one can see the kingdom of God unless he is born again." J. Vernon McGee makes this comment about conversion: "Oh you can bluff your way through. You can't know heartfelt obedience until your heart has been converted." (115)

Have you ever known someone who claimed to be a Christian but kept it well hidden by his or her lifestyle?

1 John has a description for those people. In 1 John 2:4, he says, "The man who says, 'I know Him,' but does not do His commands is a liar and the truth is not in him." In Matthew 7:16, Jesus makes this statement about such people: "By their fruit you will recognize them. Do people pick grapes from thorn bushes, or figs from thistles?"

Jesus described authentic disciples as salt and light.

"You are the salt of the earth. But if the salt loses its saltiness, how can it be made salty again? It is no longer good for anything, except to be thrown out and trampled by men "You are the light of the world. A city on a hill cannot be hidden." (115)

Obedience is following the example of Jesus

Christ set the example for love. John informs us that, "Whoever claims to live in him must walk as Jesus did" (1 John 2:6).

Jesus commanded his disciples to: "Love one another. As I have loved you so you must love one another" (John 13:34). A few chapters later he gave them an example of love: "Greater love has no one than this; that he lay down his life for his friends" (John 15:13).

For far too many individuals, the word love is used in a useless or negligent way. For some it is a word that is thrown around without even considering the implication of its use. We say we love chocolate cake, we say we love someone to make them feel good or to get something from them.

Love is often used as a noun and it is—but it is more than a noun. I, probably inappropriately, use the phrase "pregnant noun" to describe it because it seems to me, any time the word is used it has a sense of some sort of action or intended behavior on the part of the one who is saying it. For God, it was a very pregnant noun. We are told in John 3:16 NKJV, "For God so loved the world that He gave His one and only Son, that whosoever believes in Him shall not perish but have eternal life."

Christ set the example for humility. Paul, the apostle informed the church of Philippi, "And being found in appearance as a man, he humbled himself and became obedient to death—even death on the cross" (Philippians 2:8a)

The *International Standard Bible Encyclopedia* points out that, "Paul makes this earnest appeal to Christians that they should cherish and manifest their Lord's humility." (116)

Much conversation is heard about humility, but it seems to me, it doesn't get enough emphasis among Christians. The Bible teaches in many places throughout that humility is a special mark of Christianity. In the *International Standard Bible Encyclopedia*, it is pointed out that, "In the Old Testament and in the New Testament, humility is an essential characteristic of true piety, or of the man who is right with God." (117)

Christ set the example for obedience. In Philippians 2:8b, the Bible says he "became obedient unto death."

How far are you willing to go in your effort to do the will of God? Perhaps he is calling you to a special task right now. Are you willing to do as he asks?

Two years ago, my wife and I felt God calling us to a church in New Mexico. Our home in Oklahoma is almost five hundred miles away so we had to sell most of our stuff, including animals, and gave the rest away.

Our ministry there was strongly opposed by one who had convinced most of the church he was right even though the Bible proved he was wrong. We really took a beating and finally came home to allow them to find another solution.

When we arrived home, we went to a local church the next Sunday morning, the Pastor said to me, "I bet you don't do that again." My response was, "If God calls me, I will."

We were called to a church almost two hundred miles from here last year and had a very joyful and fulfilling experience. If he calls again, I'm ready. (118)

Please forgive the personal story, but I told it, not to bring attention to myself, but to point out the need for readiness to follow the example of Christ wherever he leads. Many missionaries and pastors and other Christians have given up much more and have done much more. I'm sure they, as I do, give the glory to God.

Light for walking on the path of righteousness reveals love for others. Love for others Is Evidence of Salvation. 1 John 2:10 informs us: "Whoever loves his brother lives in the light and there is nothing in him to make him stumble."

Like the lawyer in Matthew who asked Jesus, "Who is my neighbor?" some would ask, "Who is my brother?" Jesus answered the question with a parable that has a broad implication that is also be said of brotherhood.

"Who is my brother? "Whosoever shall do the will of God, the same is my brother and sister, and my mother" (Mark 3:35).

Baker's Dictionary of Theology tells us: "With the emergence of the nation Israel, the term came to mean fellow countrymen." Jesus, on the other hand, "magnified two criteria. If one were prepared to do the will of God, he would be recognized as a brother by the Lord. All those who recognize Jesus as their leader and teacher become brethren by that acknowledgement." (119)

He further states, "It is clear from the book of Acts and from the epistles, that 'brethren' was a common mode of designation for fellow believers." Although the term as it is used in the Bible applies to spiritual brotherhood in the general sense that should not preclude our loving others with whom we come in contact. (120)

It is at least as important to express our love in our actions toward all mankind as it is to recognize our spiritual brothers and sisters in Christ. That means we should express that love all the time everywhere.

If there is a need to express a universal love, there is a need to explain how we can accomplish that task.

Gracious Behavior Is a Revelation of Christian Love

Often others are rude or selfish in our presence. When that happens, the love of Christ should motivate Christians to be channels of Godly grace. One definition of grace is "unearned mercy." All of us find ourselves in a position of need for that from time to time. After all, it was by his unearned mercy that Christ saved us despite our sins and shortcomings.

Liberal giving to one in need is a revelation of Christian love, but not all who claim to be a Christian realize that. One example of that was an experience I had several years ago, while stationed in Germany.

I was stationed at Baumholder, Germany, for a short time before my wife came to join me. During that time, I was sent from Baumholder to Mannheim—about ninety miles away—for helicopter maintenance training.

Trinity Baptist Church of Baumholder asked me to preach for them one Sunday evening while I was living in Mannheim.

Since I was of very low pay status and had five children, our budget was very tight, but I decided to drive the ninety miles anyway even though my old Plymouth Savoy was a gas hog and almost out of gas. I mistakenly thought they might give me some money for driving ninety miles to preach that service. They didn't. I was broke and out of gas. I was faced with a dilemma. My only hope was to borrow enough money to buy gas to get back to Mannheim.

One of the church members was a major in the army. I asked him for a loan. He did loan me five dollars, but with the loan came a long lecture on the management of my money. I only travelled a little over halfway when I ran out of gas. Maybe there was some grace in there somewhere. I guess he could have said no. (121)

John makes this comment about benevolence: "If anyone has material possessions and sees his brother has need but has no pity on him, how can the love of God be in him?" (1 John 3:17 NIV).

Then he offers this very definitive advice: "Dear children, let us not love with words or tongue but with actions and in truth" (1 John 3:18 NIV).

CHAPTER 9

Light on the Path of Righteousness Reveals Forbidden Love

1 John 2:15–17

I feel driven by honesty and the love of God to begin this segment with the confession that I have been guilty of many of the forbidden loves John has pointed out in the King James Version of the Bible at one time or the other. It is my constant prayer that I will not find myself guilty again.

Knowing that every temptation crouches at the door of my life experiences and my relationship with God and the world; I know and can identify with the apostle Paul when he said in Romans 7:15, "For what I want to do, I do not do, but what I hate I do."

The struggle between sin and righteousness is a constant one that we of ourselves cannot overcome. It must be accomplished through the grace and power of Jesus Christ, the righteous one. I can further identify with Paul when he says in 1 Corinthians 7:24–25: "What a wretched man I am! Who will rescue me from this body of death? Thanks, be to God—through Jesus Christ, our Lord."

Guy H. King offers this consolation, if it can be called that: "This verse makes plain that the world draws away our love from the Father: You can't have both. Many a Christian has found that profoundly true." (122)

John confirms that very thing when he says, "If anyone loves the world, the love of the Father is not in him" (1 John 2:15).

Love of a worldly system is forbidden. 1 John 2:15, "Do not love the world," does not necessarily mean the physical world. J. Vernon McGee makes this point very well in his commentary on 1 John, "John is not talking about the physical earth where beautiful roses and tall trees grow." A few verses further down he offers this explanation. "The Greek word for *world* is cosmos. It means the world system." (125)

Virtually everyone would agree with J. Vernon McGee concerning the many beautiful sights in this world. Sin is not in their existence, but in our attitude concerning their existence.

This admonishment is not to change behavior only; it, more exactly, is a matter of the heart, mind and behavior. Because where the heart goes, the heels will follow. Our behavior is an outward manifestation of the things we believe.

It is important to remember one of the reasons John was writing this letter was to combat spiritual infidelity. The Gnostics were having a very destructive influence on Christianity because of their very unscriptural views. The *Holman Illustrated Bible Dictionary* offers this description of Gnosticism: "Some Gnostic systems took an opposite turn into antinomianism (A belief that moral law is not valid for a person or group.) They claimed that Christians were not responsible for what they did and could not really sin because their fleshly existence was not part of God's plan. Thus, they could act in any way they pleased without fear of discipline." (124)

John's answer To Gnostic doctrine is very clear: For everything in the world—the cravings of sinful man, the lust of the eyes, and boasting of what he has and does—come not from the Father but from the world. The world and its desires pass away, but the man of God lives forever." (125)

Love for worldly ways is forbidden. Numbers twenty-five might be an example for us to consider. In that situation, the Israelites began to mingle with the people of Moab and eventually to practice their idolatrous religion involving sexual acts of sacrifice among other things. God's anger was showered upon the perpetrators in that situation, similarly, John promised the people of his day punishment from God for their spiritual infidelity.

There is a trend or a perspective today of "tolerance." I have heard "Christians" say many times, "As long as you believe something, that's what's important."

Christians should be intolerant to some degree. We should be intolerant of sin. We should be intolerant of false religions, and we should be intolerant of ignorance pertaining to the Word of God. Wherever these conditions exist, Christians should become involved with a ministry of love by example, by ministry, and by teaching the word of God.

John, here, emphasizes the need to believe the right things and to live the right way: "Love not the world, neither the things in the world." It is his admonishment to return to the Holy scriptures as our guide book and follow its teaching.

Love of world is proof of being lost. Perhaps it's time for some who consider their self a Christian to examine their own behavior. Do you remember 1 John 1:6? "If we claim to have fellowship with him yet walk in darkness, we lie and do not the truth." Then repeated in 1 John 2:4 in a little different way, "The man who says, 'I know him,' but does not do what he commands is a liar, and the truth is not in him." Here, in 1 John 2:15, there is an extension of that declaration. He says in the last part of verse fifteen, "If any man love the world, the love of the Father is not in him." How is it possible to sing, "O how I love Jesus," on Sunday then serve Satan and the world the other six days of the week? In the vernacular of an old man way back in the backwoods of Alabama many years ago, "You either is or you ain't." I believe that's what John is telling us here. Jesus himself said, "No one can serve two masters" (Matthew 6:24); yet that is what many are attempting to do today.

John makes the need for spiritual fidelity very clear; "Love not the world." (1 John 2:15).

Harold T. Bryson has written a message concerning this passage titled, "Watch Your Love Life" (126) to me that is another way to say what John is telling the Christians of his day and it is just as relevant today.

The advice of John seems very harsh to many of us because we want to be popular in the world and be looked upon as one who is highly esteemed among men. The apostle Paul asks a question that should bring some perspective to those who are seeking recognition from their peers: "Where is the wise man? Where is the scholar? Where is the philosopher of this age? Has not God made foolish the wisdom of the world?" (1 Corinthians 1: 20).

In the King James Version of the Bible, there is a list of three categories or kinds of sin characterized in a general way. They are "The lust of the flesh, and the lust of the eyes, and the pride of life" (1 John 2:16). It is my intention to discuss each one of them separately and elaborate for clarification.

The Lust of the Flesh

The lust of the flesh includes more than one could list. Usually when we talk about lust, we think of it as referring to sex, and it does, but it also refers to anything else in the world we develop an inordinate desire to have.

Some lust after material things. I haven't yet understood why a couple should live in a two-story house and have three cars and an excess of whatever else they can accumulate around them unless they are searching for satisfaction of their lust to own things.

Probably the most destructive type of lust is the lust for self-glory. In some of the churches of the past there have been individuals who felt it their duty to rise during Sunday services to tell everyone what they had accomplished during the week.

In one church, there was an individual who would usually say, "The spirit lead me to witness to this many people or to an individual at Walmart" or something along that line. With all the witnessing he did, however, he never brought anybody to church. "Since I came here . . ." has been a phrase from the lips of many a pastor. Perhaps it would be more appropriate to direct the listeners to God's accomplishments.

Lust of the Flesh Is about Power

Much of the time when "Christians" talk about the "Thousand Year Reign," the conversation seems to be focused on the prospect of ruling. That attitude seems to imply a desire to be in charge. Those who are looking forward to the time when they will be in charge, in my view, have a misconception of heaven and are suffering from an inordinate desire for power. My Bible teaches that Jesus is and will be in charge. He is the power of salvation and the everlasting power of eternal life.

Have you read the qualifications of those who will reign for a thousand years with him? Revelation 20:4 describes them this way, "I saw thrones on which were seated those who had been given authority to judge. And I saw the souls of those who had been beheaded because of their testimony for Jesus and because of the word of God."

I'm sure there are those who meet those qualifications. If you are reading this, you are not one of them. You might be in the future. If you are, my prayer is that you learn to be a servant leader instead of a slave driver as the manner of some is.

Peter gives an example of being an overseer: "Be shepherds of God's flock that is under your care, serving as overseers—not because you must, but because you are willing, as God wants you to be; not greedy for money, but eager to serve. Not lording it over those entrusted to you, but being examples to the flock."(129)

No one is looking forward to the day he or she will be with Jesus more than I am, but I'm looking forward to the great and precious promises of glory land. 1 Corinthians 2:9 tells us, "Eye has not seen nor ear heard; neither has it entered into the imagination of man, the things God has in store for those who love him." My version: "What a day that will be, when my Jesus I shall see," but not because I'm in charge.

I suppose the truth of the matter is that many in and out of the church who are lusting after power, are looking for it in this present world and are willing to do whatever it takes to get it. The lust for power is a form of self-worship often brought about by feelings of insecurity or mistrust of others. If you are one of those who are looking for power or influence in or out of the church, perhaps you should seek the assurance that God loves you and then learn to be satisfied in that love.

Lust of the Flesh Is about Love of Money

Probably, one of the most misquoted verses of scripture deals with money. It is often misquoted as, "Money is the root of all evil." The actual verse is found in 1 Timothy 6:10 and the correct quote is, "For the love of money is a root of all kinds of evil." Here, once again, it is not the object that is evil but the attitude concerning it.

Poor people can be as guilty concerning the lust for riches as rich people when one considers that it is the greed, inordinate desire, or lustful love that causes sin. Anytime anything becomes more important in life than God, it is sin because it is a form of idolatry. Remember way back in Exodus 20:3 "You shall have no other gods before me." God should be the most important thing in life. What is most important to you? Can others see Jesus in you? Are you guilty of spiritual infidelity? Allow me to caution you: "Watch your love life. Do not taste of forbidden love."

The Lust of the Eyes Is the Third Topic Mentioned by John.

"It doesn't hurt to look." is a defensive statement I have heard many times from men, young and old from many places in the world, but most of us have discovered looking is the first step on the path to sin.

Guy H. King makes this observation concerning the lust of the eye, "Evil desires enter through eye gate. How many robbers of men's purity slipped through that unguarded entrance?" (128)

Genesis 3:6 informs us that, "The woman saw that the fruit of the tree was good." In other words, she looked. In Joshua 7:21, Achan said, "I saw." In Matthew 14:30, "Peter saw the wind and was afraid." Guy H. King makes a very valid point and the scriptures support it strongly. Looking is often the first step on the path to sin. (129)

The pride of life is probably the most prevalent sin in this list. The writer of proverbs claims that, "Pride goes before destruction, a haughty spirit before a fall" (Proverbs 16:18).

Have you ever known someone who seemed to have a pedestal complex? That describes one who sees himself or herself as being on a pedestal. In his commentary on 1 John 2:16, Matthew Henry calls it, "The disease of the ear," while discussing the pride of life. He further describes it as, "A vain mind which craves all the grandeur, equipage, and pomp of a vain—glorious life; this is ambition, and thirst after honor and applause." (130)

Those who suffer from this "pedestal complex" seem to be constantly saying things either by words or by action to indicate they are more special than those around them.

On the surface this kind of behavior often appears as excessive pride and can be the action of one who really does have great pride in himself and his accomplishments, but, in many cases, however, it is motivated by a sense of not being good enough in the eyes of others and, consequently, a strong desire for recognition.

The apostle Paul advised us: "Do not think of yourself more highly than you ought to think" (Romans 12:3). One of the most common sentences you might hear from one who is afflicted with the pride of life is, "Look what I've done." I have known a few Christian men and women, who were members of a committee of some kind or another, frame their report to imply or say out right. "Look what I did."

There is a desire for recognition possibly brought on by the lack thereof in the past, and the failure to realize that all they are and have is a result of God and his part in their life. It's a hard pill to swallow that without him we are nothing, but it is very clearly presented in the scriptures, and until we realize that, vanity and pride will influence all of us to one extent or another.

Pride Flaunts Position

Sometimes an individual will introduce himself or herself by title or position. Many years ago, I became a sergeant in the army. One day a young man of lower rank called me by my first name. Being the gung ho, prideful individual that I was, I turned to him and said, "My first name is Sergeant to you." What arrogance! What a bizarre presentation of pride! Of course, it embarrassed him and caused a rift in our relationship. It is true that "a haughty spirit goes before a fall."

Pride Flaunts Possession

I was called to serve as pastor of a large/small church sometime back. They had a large, magnificent building but only a few were attending. On my first visit I was escorted through the building and was informed with pride by the individual who preened with proudness, "I am very particular about how it looks." This church had over fifty thousand dollars in savings and checking, yet this individual, who was so proud of the building, objected adamantly to benevolence for local people. (133)

The World Is Temporary

The house is on fire! I heard my daughter scream over the phone.

We lived in Maize, Kansas, but had a triplex and a three-bedroom home in Wichita not far away. My daughter, her husband, and three children were living in the house.

I dressed as quickly as possible and sped over there. When I arrived, I found that the fire department had managed to put out the fire, but not before the insides were completely destroyed.

That property had been part of a dream. Not mine so much as my daughter and her husband's. Although I had bought it, they had plans to rent the triplex while living in the house and build another house on the property and sell it. That night their dream was shattered. In a few minutes, they had lost everything they owned and much I had owned. (131)

When John said, "The world and its desires pass away" (John 2:17), perhaps he had something like that burning house in mind. But there are other things of the world we fall in love with only to see them disintegrate before our eyes.

Our heavenly inheritance is permanent. It is permanent because it is an inheritance from a permanent God. When we sing, "I've got a mansion," we are singing those words because God has given us that promise.

Peter informs us in his first letter of that promise as he speaks to those who have been scattered abroad: "Praise be to the God and Father of our Lord Jesus Christ! In his great mercy, he has given us new birth into a living hope through the resurrection of Jesus Christ from the dead, and into an inheritance that can never perish, spoil or fade – kept in heaven for you." (132)

Our inheritance is permanent because God's love for us is permanent. The apostle Paul offers this assurance with these words: "In all these things, we are more than conquerors through him that loved us. For I am convinced that neither death nor life, neither angels nor demons, neither the present nor the future, nor any powers, neither height nor depth, nor anything else in all creation will be able to separate us from the love of God that is in Christ Jesus our Lord." (133)

Have you heard the phrase, "The difference between a hero and a villain is a very thin line?" So many times, for many individuals, love for someone or something has been overwhelming then, suddenly, something happened to immediately change that position.

"Love is often a word used for lust or greed or fascination with an object that leads to destruction." John said, "Love not the world neither the things that are in the world because they are temporary. His stated reason for that warning is 'The world and its desires pass away.'" (1 John 2:17)

Many years ago, when I was a child, we would sing, "Build your hopes on things eternal, hold to God's unchanging hand." Wow! What good advice. What a beautiful song. And it's so true. We didn't know what it all meant back then, and maybe we still don't. But from where I am, it is the promise that says it all. Look again at 1 John 2:17: "But the man who does the will of God lives forever."

There is a verse found in both the old and the new testaments that summarizes this message about love: "Love the Lord your God with all your heart and with all your soul and with all your mind" (Matthew 22:37). If we set that verse as a standard and live by it we will not wander into forbidden love.

Pride flaunts knowledge. One of the differences between Christianity and Gnosticism was their perspective concerning knowledge. The Gnostics had concluded that knowledge trumped faith. The Holman Illustrated Bible Dictionary tells us, "The Gnostics thought faith was inferior to knowledge. The true sons of the absolute deity were saved through knowledge rather than faith." (134)

I once had the experience of knowing a director of missions in a Southern Baptist Association who insisted he be addressed as doctor. I made the mistake of addressing him as brother, and he informed me that part of his agreement with that association was that he be addressed as *doctor*. Most of us who have done extensive study or have attained or both, some level of scholastic recognition understand the effort involved in that accomplishment. But by the same token, most of us realize whatever knowledge or accomplishment we have is due to God's grace and in response to his call. I have known, as I'm sure many of you have, men and women of great stature in the world of academia, or some other area or field of endeavor who were quite unassuming as to their level or status compared to others. (135)

CHAPTER 10

Spiritual Light Reveals Those Who Are the Antichrist

1 John 2:18–27

Some have apparently degenerated from lovers of the world to Antichrist. J. Vernon McGee tells us, "Antichrist is made up of two words. The title *Christ* and the preposition *anti*. It is important to see that *anti* has two meanings. It can mean *against*. If I am anti something, it means I'm against that thing. *Anti* can also mean *instead of*—an imitation of. Therefore, it can be a substitute (136)

The writer of *The Preacher's Homiletic Commentary* on 1 John says, "Whatever in the church opposes the living authority and rule of the Lord Jesus is an antichrist." (137)

From the information found in commentaries and in 1 John 2:18–20, we can see two factions working against the gospel: There are the Gnostics who are opposed to the teachings of the apostles and those who fell in love with the world and dropped out. All of those involved with those perspectives have received this warning from Christ himself: "He who is not with me is against me and he who does not gather with me scatters" (Matthew 12:30).

Longevity is a sign of authenticity. John points out one of the ways an authentic Christian can be recognized when he says, "They went out from us, but they were not of us" (1 John 2:19 NKJV).

It is not so uncommon in churches today to see individuals drop out because they don't like the preacher or something he said or something someone else said. Perhaps that is because they have unrealistic expectations; it is expected by some, that joining the church will solve life's problems for them, but as you will see later, happiness does not always come from joining a church when they find that to be the case, they begin looking for another solution.

Jesus is the solution! Authenticity is only available to the individual who yields his or her life to Jesus Christ and accepts him as Lord and Savior.

This world will always have its share of sorrow and disappointments therefore it is imperative that joy come from the indwelling Christ and his promise of everlasting life in paradise. The apostle Paul pointed that out in 1 Corinthians 15:19 when he said, "If only for this life we have hope in Christ, we are to be pitied more than all men."

John points out the lack of authenticity in those who had left the fellowship when he says, "For if they had belonged to us, they would have remained with us." (1 John 2:19).

Jesus offered an example of those who come and go in the parable of the sower.

"Then He spoke many things to them in parables, saying: 'Behold, a sower went out to sow. And as he sowed, some seed fell by the wayside; and the birds came and devoured them. Some fell on stony places, where they did not have much earth; and they immediately sprang up because they had no depth of earth. But when the sun was up they were scorched, and because they had no root they withered away. And some fell among thorns, and the thorns sprang up and choked them. But others fell on good ground and yielded a crop: some a hundred- fold, some sixty and some thirty. He who has ears let him hear!" (138)

Another example of longevity is the tree planted beside the water mentioned by the writer of Psalms:

"Blessed is the man who walks not in the counsel of the ungodly, nor stands in the path of sinners, nor sits in the seat of the scornful; But his delight is in the law of the Lord, and in his law, he meditates day and night. He shall be like a tree Planted by the rivers of water, that brings forth its fruit in its season, whose leaf also shall not wither; and whatever he does shall prosper." (139)

These three statements about longevity support the statement made above by John. Although it is not the only factor in the identity of authentic Christians, longevity is one confirmation of authenticity.

Is it possible that inactive church members are Antichrist?

Although there are exceptions, there are many who are unable to be involved for one reason or another, many of those who are described by John as Antichrist bear a striking resemblance to those we call inactive church members. In 1 John 2:19, he put it this way. "They went out from us but they really did not belong to us."

J. Vernon McGee gives us a *Parable of the Pig* and relates it to 2 Peter 2:22, "A little girl pig went up to the Father's house, became very religious, got all cleaned up with a pink bow around her neck and her teeth brushed with Pepsodent, but she didn't like the father's house because she was a pig, so one day she said, 'I'm going to rise and go to my father, my old man.' Her old man was down in a big loblolly of mud. The little pig went home and when she saw her old man, she squealed, made a leap, and landed in the mud right beside him. Why? Because she was a pig. 'It would have been better for them not to have known the way of righteousness, than to have known it and then to turn their backs on the sacred command that was passed on to them.' Of them, the proverbs are true: A dog returns to its vomit and a sow that is washed goes back to her wallowing in the mud" (2 Peter 2:21–22). (140)

Excuses are typical for inactive church members. In my fifty plus years in the ministry, I have heard a multitude of them. "Someone said this or that and hurt my feelings," "I don't like the preacher," "I don't have time," "I'm too busy," and the list goes on. There is one constant, however, in all these complaints: it is the word *I*. It is my observation and the observation of many others that *I* is the letter in the middle of the word sin.

For authentic Christians, excuses give way to Christian priorities. Christian priorities are declared by Christ and repeated and made clear by the apostles. They are: Christ first, others second, and self last. Jesus made it very clear: "Anyone who loves his father and mother more than me is not worthy of me; anyone who loves his son or daughter more than me is not worthy of me; and anyone who does not take up his cross and follow me is not worthy of me." (141)

Distractions create excuses. It is easy to become distracted. We have discussed the pride of life and the lust of the eye. Both are preludes to becoming ambivalent about church. Genesis 3:1 warns us that, "Satan is the sneakiest beast in the field," we could also add that he is the source of many distractions.

Excuses often involve scapegoats. We can blame it on Satan, our neighbor, an attractive individual we met or some other excuse. But John says very clearly, "If they had belonged to us, they would have remained with us."

Longevity equals authenticity. Those who are described in 1 John 2:19 are the seeds that took no root in Jesus's parable of the sower Matthew 13:5 and represent those who fit the definition offered by J. Vernon McGee as "an imitation without authenticity." (142)

There is another type of Antichrist to consider, however, they are those who actively oppose biblical doctrine, disrupt the church and cause confusion among Christians in the church. These individuals are indicated as one of the purposes for this writing: "I am writing these things to you about those who are trying to lead you astray" (1 John 2:26). Some of them belong to various religious organizations and, just as the Gnostics did in John's day, are very active in their opposition to Christianity.

Apostates who had found their position within the church impossible, so had left the church, and were now making themselves as actively mischievous against the church as they possibly could.

"A little further down he makes this statement: "And such persons are antichrists in every age." (143)

Some believe opposition from other religions are the great danger to the church, and that is possibly true, but it is my position that the greatest danger comes from those who claim Christianity but are actively involved in the destruction of its framework and denouncing the Bible as the infallible word of God. These are those who, in the words of the *Preacher's Homiletic Commentary* are: "Those who wanted to make Christianity an opinion rather than life." (144)

One type of the Antichrist that is condoned and overlooked is found in the field of secular education. When I was attending Northwestern Oklahoma State University in the eighties, the Bible was found in the mythological section. Prayer has been banned from schools and school activities by law. Those who continue that activity are persecuted for it in many cases. Those brave and faithful servants deserve to be commended for their actions, I'm sure they are, by our Holy Father.

While denigrating the Bible and Christianity, many are quite busy promoting the alternative to creation known as the theory of evolution. Although their position is riddled with fallacy and unprovable supposition, they attempt to claim it as fact. It is more accurately described by many as, "A hoax perpetrated upon the world."

Confession is a sign of authenticity. John offers this assurance to authentic Christians, "Whoever acknowledges the Son has the Father also" (1 John 2:23). On the other hand, he informs us, "No one who denies the Son has the Father; whoever acknowledges the son, has the Father also."

This is clearly the reason for the test of spiritual authenticity. It is why it is so important for those who present the gospel to emphasize the complete formula for salvation as described by the apostle Paul in Romans 10:9: "That if you confess with your mouth that Jesus is Lord, and believe in your heart that God raised him from the dead, you will be saved."

Authenticity is important. The importance of authenticity is confirmed in Romans 10:10 when Paul informs us, "For it is with the heart that you believe and are justified, and it is with your mouth that you confess and are saved." Jesus says, "He who confesses me before men, I will confess before the Father."

Confession of our faith involves both behavior and declaration. We are reminded in 2 Timothy 2:19b NIV, "The Lord knows those who are his, and everyone who confesses the name of the Lord must turn away from wickedness."

Behavior Is a Testimony of Conversion

John makes the difference very clear when he says: "Whoever believes in the Son has eternal life, but whoever rejects the Son will not see life but God's wrath abides on him" (John 3:36). So then, it comes down to this, either you believe or you don't.

Behavior Is a Measure of Authenticity

What you do is what you believe. If you are living a life that glorifies Satan and sin, that's what you believe. It's not enough to say you believe there is a God. The writer of Hebrews informs us that: "Anyone who comes to him must believe that he exists" (Hebrews 11:6). But that isn't the whole story; he goes on to say, "He rewards those who earnestly seek him"

John makes the very pertinent point that: "No one who denies the Son has the Father; whoever acknowledges the Son has the Father also" (1 John2:23).

The word *acknowledge* is another way to say confession. Jesus told the disciples, "Everyone, therefore, who shall confess me before men, I shall confess before my father who is in heaven" (Matthew 10:32 NASB).

Behavior That Is Contrary to His Word Is a Form of Denial

The most obvious way to deny Christ is to become actively involved in behavior that is contrary to his word and his teachings. That's what the Gnostics were doing in the time this scripture was written. There is also another way; that is by being silent about your faith. Jesus made it very clear in Matthew 28:19–20 that our mission is to tell others.

There is no such thing as being neutral. Jesus himself said, "He that is not for me is against me."

There is a certain group of people today who call revealing their sexual orientation publicly in celebration, "Coming out of the closet." The only time a Christian should be in that kind of closet is for prayer. In Matthew 6:6, Jesus repeatedly pointed out that a Christian has the duty of telling others about him. For most authentic Christians, that is one of the great pleasures of the faith.

Authenticity includes a special anointing. John offers great hope for those who are authentically saved because they have a special anointing. In John 2:20, he tells the church, "But you have an anointing from the Holy One and all of you know the truth."

Learning is information that becomes a part of you and changes your behavior. Those individuals John spoke of who had gone out had never really learned Christ. They had never put on Christ.

CHAPTER 11

Light on the Path of Righteousness Reveals a Special Anointing Called Unction

1 John 2:20

Unction is the anointing hand of Jesus at work. John reminded those to whom he was writing, "You have an anointing from the Holy one" (1 John 2:20).

This is one of the most crucial verses in this epistle. It separates the sheep from the goats. It separates those who joined the church from those who have received the anointing of the Holy One. It separates the authentic Christian from those who "were never with us." Jesus said, "I am the good Shepherd; I know my sheep and my sheep know me" (John 10:14).

He makes identification definitively clear in verse twenty-seven of that same chapter when he says, "My sheep listen to my voice; I know them and they follow me."

The word *anoint* (*unction* in the KJV) is defined in the *Holman Illustrated Bible Dictionary* by this description: "The Hebrew verb *Mashach* (noun for *Messiah*) and the Greek word *Chrio* (noun for *Christos*) are translated "to anoint." From ancient times the priests and kings were ceremonially anointed as a sign of official appointment to office and as a symbol of God's power upon them." (145)

After extensive explanation and examples, it is further said, "Christians see Jesus as God's anointed one, the Savior."

When Peter was called to take his saving message to Cornelius, he included this statement in his message: "You know what has happened throughout Judea, beginning in Galilee after that John preached—how God anointed Jesus of Nazareth with the Holy Spirit and power and how he went around doing good and healing all who were under the power of the devil, because God was with him." (146)

The same symbolism as in the Old Testament is employed in this usage. God's presence and power are present in the anointing. The Christian is anointed by God in the case of salvation. That is confirmed by the apostle Paul when he says: "Now he who establishes us with you in Christ and has anointed us is God who also has sealed us and given us his Spirit in our hearts as a guarantee" (2 Corinthians 1:21 NKJV).

Perhaps the point can be made without stretching it too far, that the anointing mentioned in 1 John 2:20 can be related to or can be considered in the group of words that indicate a dedication or a setting apart for the purposes of God.

The definition for sanctification and consecration, meaning set aside or set apart, could be the objective of anointment, if not in fact synonymous since they have similar root words in Greek. If that is the case, authentic Christians should consider themselves saints since the definition for all these words are derived from the Greek word *Hagios*.

In his sermon of the evening at First Baptist Church, Enid, Oklahoma, Richard Stephens preached a message explaining sainthood and making the point that Saints are called by God, separated for worshipping and serving God, and set apart from the things and the destination of the world. (147)

I must have the audacity to disagree with such a great man as William Barclay where he says in his commentary on chapter fifteen of the gospel of John.

"In this passage, there is much about abiding in Christ. What is meant by that? It is true that there is a mystical sense in which the Christian is in Christ and Christ is in the Christian. But there are

113

many-maybe they are the majority- who never has experienced this mystical experience. If we are like that, we must not blame ourselves. There is a much simpler way of looking at this. It is a way open to everyone." (148)

I continued to read the commentary of William Barclay, hoping to read about God's grace and his initiative as demonstrated by the anointing spoken of by John in this epistle and by other epistles by Paul, Peter, and others, but he spent the next two pages on keeping in close contact with Jesus as another way of salvation. I have spent over thirty years working, sleeping, eating, and playing with the American Indian people. One member of my family has informed me that my great-grandfather was a Cherokee. That is not proved, but if it is true, I have inherited a Cherokee bloodline just as in my new birth I spiritually inherited Jesus's bloodline. My very best friend and mentor is a Creek Indian. I have preached in his church, and he has preached in mine several times. With all that close association, however, I have not become Creek, Pawnee, or Cheyenne.

On page 176 of his commentary on John, Barclay continues, "For some few of us abiding in Christ will be a mystical experience." His word *mystical* is open to interpretation or clarification at least. He continues with these words of explanation: "Which is beyond words to express. For most of us, it will mean a constant contact with him. It will mean arranging life, arranging prayer, arranging silence in such a way that there is never a day when we give ourselves a chance to forget him." (149)

Apparently, William Barclay, along with Nicodemus, misunderstood the words of Jesus: "I tell you the truth, no one can see the kingdom of God unless he is born again" (John 3:3); Or perhaps the words of Paul when he said, "Not of works, lest any man should boast" (Ephesians 2:9); or earlier, when Paul declares: "In him we have redemption through his blood, the forgiveness of sins, in accordance with the riches of God's grace" (Ephesians 1:7). Paul reveals his perspective to us through his testimony: "I have been crucified with Christ and I no longer live, but Christ lives in me. The life I now live in the body, I live by faith in the Son of God, who loved me and gave himself for me" (Galatians 2:20).

The word (unction) is realized as a spiritual anointing. It's not about us! It's not about works! It's about being a branch of the vine. Just as the condemnation for sin flowed from Adam, so the salvation from Jesus Christ flows into the spiritual veins of every real Christian. Jesus said, "I am the vine, you are the branches" (John 15:5).

I am part of the family of God. I have a heavenly Father! I haven't earned the right to be in the family; I don't deserve to be in the family. It is only because of his amazing grace that he called me out, cleaned me up, and gave me everlasting life. His anointing verifies that. It might or might not be "mystical" but it's real.

The anointing John speaks of is a gift from God. To continue and elaborate on the point made above, the anointing John speaks of in 1 John 2:20 is a spiritual anointing. It is neither delivered nor contaminated by the handling of man. John makes the point that it's "from the Holy One." I understand that to mean from Christ Jesus through the Holy Spirit he promised in John 16:5–11.

It is an anointing for spiritual equipment and blessing. This is the anointing that offers the power of the anointed to discern between the professors and the possessors. John tells those "little children" that "I do not write to you because you do not know the truth, but because you know it" (1 John 2:21).

It is not the laying on of hands, although that ceremony has its purpose. It is not pouring water or oil on an individual's head although there are those who claim those ceremonies serve a purpose. This is an anointing of the heart. This is the spiritual appointment of God to service along with the equipping and the blessings that go along with it.

It is an anointing for spiritual strength and endurance. The anointing John speaks of in 1 John 2:27 not only affirms the purpose of discernment pointed out in verse twenty; it goes on to furnish Christians the strength to remain in all things. In other words, it also furnishes staying power.

Many who call themselves Christians drop out because their unrealistic expectations are not met or because their self is the center of their universe, they begin looking elsewhere for fulfillment.

The apostle Paul informed us, "If only for this life we have hope in Christ, we are pitied more than all men" (1 Corinthians 15:19). I'm not to be pitied! No matter what the world has in store for me, I have a home in glory land.

My Bible tells me: "No eye has seen, nor ear heard, no mind has conceived what God has prepared for those who love him" (1 Corinthians 2:9). I believe it and am looking forward to the day I can claim it. John strongly expresses that same desire when he says: "And now, dear children, continue in him, so that when he appears we may be confident and unashamed before him at his coming" (1 John 2:28).

CHAPTER 12

Light on the Path of Righteousness Reveals the Greatness of God's Love

1 John 3:1

The very first thing we should notice about the love of God is its greatness. That greatness is pointed out in 1 John 3:1a: "How great is the love the Father has lavished on us."

For men and nature greatness is measured several different ways. George Washington was great because of his accomplishments. Billy Graham is considered great because of his accomplishments. The Rocky Mountains are considered great because of their size and scope. The list could go on indefinitely, but there is nothing, nor anyone, whose greatness can be compared to the greatness of God or the greatness of his love.

God's word to Moses and to the people of Israel as he prepared to give them the Ten Commandments is a description of his greatness and the greatness of his love for those who love him: "I, the Lord your God, am a jealous God, punishing the children of the fathers to the fourth generation of those who hate me, but showing love to a thousand generations of those who love me and keep my commandments." (150)

Jeremiah confirms that the love of God is great because it is everlasting when he states, "The Lord appeared to us in the past saying: 'I have loved you with an everlasting love; I have drawn you with loving kindness'" (Jeremiah 31:3).

God's love has been present from the beginning. "With everlasting kindness, I will have compassion on you, says the Lord your redeemer" (Isaiah 54:8). The words of God express a desire for love toward us when he said, "Let us make man in our image, in our likeness" (Genesis 1:26). His promise to Abram while he was still in Mesopotamia was an expression of love to his chosen people.

The rescue of Israel from Egypt was an expression of his love. The several times Israel failed and was saved by the hand of God are all expressions of his love and his ultimate plan to express his ultimate love through the sacrifice of his only begotten Son for the salvation of all mankind.

John gives us the assurance God's love will ultimately be revealed in glory in the following statement, "Dear friends, now we are children of God, and what we will be has not yet been made known. But we know that when he appears, we shall be like him, for we shall see him as he is."

There are those who have great hopes for riches, others hope and struggle for popularity. Others hope for abundant worldly things; but the great hope for all authentic Christians is the hope that one day we will see Jesus and be as he is. The church members at Thessalonica were discussing that very thing when Paul gave them this exciting answer: "The resurrection of Jesus from the grave is a shadow or a forecast of the resurrection of all" (1 Thessalonians 4:13–17).

The apostle Paul assures them and us: "But Christ has indeed been raised from the dead, the first fruits of those who have fallen asleep" (1 Corinthians 15:20)

God's love is available everywhere today. That the Love of God is everywhere is emphasized repeatedly by John. It is made clear by a verse many of us memorized as children: "For God so loved the world that he gave his one and only Son that whosoever believes in him shall not perish but have eternal life" (John 3:16). Look again at that verse. It begins with the words: "For God so loved the world."

In 1961, I was guarding a small Cessna aircraft in a remote part of the country of South Korea. To my knowledge, no one was in the area but me and the airplane.

Suddenly, a nine- or ten-year-old Korean girl appeared out of the bushes surrounding the location. I could, at that time, speak a limited amount of Korean, so I began to talk to her about Jesus in Korean. This is her response to my question: "Nay Yesu sarang, Nay Yesu sarang, Nay Yesu sarang. Yesu sarang hasim to." Translated as, "Yes, Jesus loves me, yes, Jesus loves me. Yes, Jesus loves me, the Bible tells me so." Those words might not be correct because it has been over forty years since that occasion, but they touched my heart and life and still do. (151)

That is only one of the many occasions where I have personally witnessed the universal love of Christ. I have found it in Germany, Japan, and Korea and even in Vietnam.

God's love is great because of universal outreach. Southern Baptists alone have more than four thousand nine hundred fifty-two missionaries around the world spreading God's great love in places many of us have never heard of, sometimes despite great danger and deprivation. Many of those who can't go send money. One hundred seventy-five million dollars were given as an expression of love for missions by Southern Baptists in the year 2011 alone. I'm sure other denominations and organizations have given vast amounts of money and manpower I am not aware of. This is concrete evidence of the universality of God's great love.

The greatest thing about God's great love is that it is personal. 1 John 3:1 uses the phrase, "The Father has lavished on us."

It is one thing to say, "For God so loved the world." It is quite another to say, "For God so loved us," and even a greater thing to be able to say, "He loves me," yet Jesus tells us, "Even the hairs of our head are numbered."

The hymn we sometimes sing in church, "Whosoever surely meaneth me," probably explains the personal emphasis God has placed on his love. The apostle Paul uses a personalizing word when he says: "Therefore, since we have been justified through faith, we have peace with God through our Lord Jesus Christ" (Romans 5:1).

God's love is great because it is available to everyone. For some, it seems difficult to accept the invitation God has delivered to all people everywhere for their own reasons, both psychological and spiritual, but that difficulty is the result of their not knowing the greatness of it.

Because a call to salvation is a call to surrender, many individuals refuse to humble themselves before the throne of grace, but it is imperative that humility be a part of acceptance of that call, without humility and subsequent surrender, salvation is impossible.

Others feel God will not save them because of their social position. Perhaps relating a mission effort we enjoyed in Virginia will reveal the fallacy of that claim.

We were stationed at Fort Lee Virginia in 1972. We had just returned from a tour of duty overseas and were getting established when the director of missions for that association informed us of a "chapel" operating just outside of Hopewell.

We drove out on Sunday morning to look and get acquainted. The total attendance was one older lady and six children from the community in ragged shorts, halter tops, etc. River Road Baptist Chapel was a three-bedroom house with folding chairs in the living room and a makeshift podium in the kitchen.

The lady asked me if I would preach for them. I said I would without hesitation because I believe a preacher should be ready to preach or die at a moment's notice and practice it.

When I had finished the message, and begun the invitation, she named a couple of the children and told them, "It's time for you to get saved." We counseled with them then waited for a time when they could make their own decision.

We baptized several people in the year or so we were there and grew to sixty in attendance with very little income except that which came from me and a few military personnel who had joined.

At the end of that short time, however, God moved the army to move me to Fort Rucker Alabama. (152)

Whatever happened at River Road Baptist Chapel happened because God was at work among those young men and women. Almost no one had any money to speak of, but they had a hunger for God and that is a strong motivator for one to come to Christ and salvation.

God is eager to save you regardless of your social situation if you sincerely intend to make a decision for him and allow him to change you and anoint you into the kingdom.

God's love is great in its results. Because of God's great love, he made a way for us to become his children. John says it like this: "How great is the love the Father has lavished on us, that we should be called the children of God" (1 John 3:1b). That is an act that only he can perform.

Everything we are and believe comes from the experience of rebirth. No matter how many good works one does, or how much money is donated to the church or worthy causes, unless you have accepted God's loving forgiveness and been born again, you are still bound for everlasting destruction. That point was made very clear when it was written in Revelation 20:15: "If anyone's name was not found written in the book of life, he was thrown in the lake of fire."

Because of his great love, he made us heirs and it is a great thing to say we are heirs of the kingdom of God but the Bible says we are more than heirs. We are told: "No eye has seen, nor ear heard, no mind has conceived what God has prepared for those who love him" (1 Corinthians 2:9). It is great to sing, "I've got a mansion just over the hilltop" and other songs about the promises of God, but I am clinging to 1 Corinthians 2:9 and saying, "Glory is indescribable!" It is made possible because God loves me.

CHAPTER 13

Light Is Revealed to God's Children by the Holy Spirit on the Path of Righteousness

1 John 3:1–2

The apostle Paul declares to us that God's children have an inheritance, "The Spirit Himself bears witness with our spirit that we are children of God, and if children, then heirs- heirs of God and joint heirs with Christ" (Romans 8:16–17a)

Now if we are children, there are conditions to that inheritance. Authenticity is one of the conditions for inheritance. We must identify with Christ in this present world and we must be prepared to suffer the scorn and abuse of the world brought on by their fear of the unknown. Paul says, "Now if we are children then we are heirs and joint heirs with Christ if indeed we share in his sufferings in order that we may also share in his glory" (Romans 8:17b).

Contending with ignorance is part of being an authentic Christian. Ignorance is defined as a state of not knowing or lack of knowledge.

The world does not know God. "The reason the world does not know us is that it did not know him" (1 John 3:1). Therefore, those who are of the world behave in a way that is without that spiritual guidance that comes from knowing God. This ignorance accounts for the destructive behavior in the name of fun and becoming involved in useless activities to pass the time or to entertain a desire that cannot be satisfied by worldly activities.

Contending with worldly pride and attitudes is part of being an authentic Christian. Because, as previously discussed, self is the center of the one who is of the world, there is a defensive attitude called pride.

Many consider pride an aggressive attitude but for the most part it is more accurately defensive. Usually the prideful person contends that they don't want to be indebted to another person or they must always be first or have the finest or some other excuse that suggests they find their worth in ownership; ownership of self or ownership of something.

Pride is often a manifestation of fear, fear of rejection, or fear of losing possession. The Bible teaches us that pride goes before a fall but faith builds confidence. Not in self or something, but in an everlasting God.

The sad side of this picture is they often believe they have found the worldly answer then they begin to swell up with pride and sometimes even treat Christians in a condescending manner. That condescension can be revealed in destructive attitudes and behavior.

Authentic Conversion Is an Absolute Requirement for Inheritance

Much of the material covered so far in 1 John has dealt with identifying with Jesus.

It is no chore for many of us to go to the front of the congregation and whisper in the ear of a pastor or counselor, but the proof of the sincerity of our confession is to be found in the life we live. While it is true that works does not save but the grace of God, it is also true, as taught throughout this study and clearly a part of biblical teaching that authentic conversion is a change of heart, a change of mind, and a change of behavior.

Christian love is evidence of authentic conversion. If we are indeed children of God, love should be at least some part of the evidence. We are directed by the Scriptures to "Walk in love, as Christ has also loved us" (Ephesians 5:2). We are instructed by Peter to live a holy life: "But just as he who called you is holy, so be holy in all you do" (1 Peter 1:15).

Jesus, himself, tells us to, "Be perfect, therefore, as your heavenly Father is perfect" (Matthew 5:48).

Guy H. King makes this point in his commentary on 1 John. He says, "Even the people of the world expect Christians to be a little Christ like, and accuse us of the lack of it." (153)

Changed behavior is evidence of authentic conversion. I would like to talk about a sensitive subject many messengers would rather not talk about to any great extent. That is spiritual freeloaders.

In Ephesians 2:10, Paul tells us, "For we are God's workmanship, created in Christ Jesus to do good works, which God prepared in advance for us to do."

Those who have voiced a profession of faith and continued walking the worldly path and not have become involved in Christian worship are living in direct disobedience to the will of God and therefore living in sin. They were called for a purpose, to worship, and to serve. If they aren't doing that, they are identifying with the philosophy and the practice of the Gnostics John was so adamantly opposed to and free loading or shirking the responsibility of their calling.

In Ephesians 4:1, Paul urges the Ephesians to "live a life worthy of the calling you have received."

The Bible repeatedly and often makes it clear that salvation is conversion. If you have not been converted, that is changed; then you are not saved.

John repeatedly points out that that Christians are different: "The reason the world does not know us is that it did not know him" (1 John 3:1). In Matthew 25:41–46, Jesus addresses the difference in authenticity and the lack of it and the consequences thereof several times during his earthly ministry.

Jesus said, "By their fruits you shall know them." How about your fruit? If you went on trial today for being a Christian, what evidence could you produce?

Paul says: "That if you confess with your mouth, Jesus is Lord, and believe in your heart that God raised him from the dead, you will be saved" (Romans 10:9). That heart thing is important because where your heart goes, your heels will follow. Have you really and sincerely and totally accepted Jesus as your Lord and Savior?

God's Children Have Special Identity

We have a present identity as we live out our life among those with whom we live and associate ourselves.

The moment we are saved we become a new person in Christ Jesus. 2 Corinthians 5:17 points out this very pertinent fact: "Therefore, if anyone is in Christ, he is a new creation, the old has gone; the new has come."

The heart that was bitter or world centered and opposed to God and godly interests before, now turns toward those things that pertain to Christ and Christianity.

The mind that was filled with mischievousness and worldly goals and objectives now turns to Christ and Christian goals and objectives.

The behavior that was involved in worldly affairs and activities now turns to activities that glorify the name of Jesus.

Many believe that a change of behavior can be a slow incremental process. To some extent that must be true, insofar as learning and behavior are concerned, but the direction will surely change. The sinful things you once endorsed and practiced are now contrary to your desires and activities. You are a new person in Christ. Your life now belongs to Jesus. You are immediately, upon conversion, a child of God: You now have a new Father, a new family, and a new future.

Christians have a future identity. John tells us it can't be presently known: "And what we will be is not yet made known" (1 John 3:2). The apostle Paul puts it this way: "Now we see but a poor reflection as in a mirror; then we shall see face to face. Now I know in part; then I shall know fully, even as I am fully known" (1 Corinthians 13:12).

The claim of Paul the Apostle in 1 Corinthians 2:9 rings throughout the discussion concerning the future blessings of the children of God, and there are, also, pictures drawn in other verses of scripture illustrating those promises.

Although we are not able to fully grasp the significance of those promises now, we can look at each one with great hope and exhilaration, knowing they will someday be ours.

The voracious appetite of many Christians to rule during the millennium is neither scriptural nor Christian.

The lust for power is committing the sin of idolatry. It is the same attitude the two brothers had in Matthew, when their mother asked Jesus to give them a position of prestige.

The King of kings and Lord of lords came into this world as a suffering servant we should expect no more or no less. It's not about power now or later; it's about being with Jesus, the author and finisher of our faith.

Christians can rejoice to the extent we can absorb and experience the things God has in store for those who love him. John offers this picture into the future for those who are indeed God's children: "They will be his people, and God himself will be with them and be their God. He will wipe away every tear from their eyes. There will be no more death or mourning or crying or pain, for the old order of things has passed away." (154)

But how do we know what it is to be like him in his resurrection body?

J. Vernon McGee makes this attempt at explanation, "We are not going to be equal to him, but we are going to be like him in our own way. This does not mean that all of us are going to be little robots or simply duplicates—it is not that at all. We will be like him with our own personalities, our own individualities, our own selves. He will never destroy the person that you are, but he is going to bring you up to full measure, the stature where you will be like him -not identical to him, but like him." (155)

I wish I could say amen to everything he said, but then I would be speculating, so I'm just going to confess ignorance and trust God's word.

Paul does make this information known: "When you sow, you do not plant that will be, but just a seed, perhaps of wheat or of something else. But God gives it a body as he has determined, and to each kind of seed he gives its own body" (1 Corinthians 15:38). Later the point is made: "It is sown a natural body, it is raised a spiritual body.

When all the speculation is over and after extensive study has been completed, the wise conclusion would be to return to 1 John 3:2. There, "Dear friends, now we are children of God, and what we will be has not yet been made known. But we know that when he appears, we shall be like him, for we shall be as he is."

CHAPTER 14

There Is Light on the Path of Righteousness to Prepare for the Lord's Day

1 John 3:3

BNSS were four letters I, and others, heard from time to time in the morning formation at the US Army Leadership Training School located at Fort Dix New Jersey. Those letters, by the way, are initials for Boots Not Spit Shined.

When we entered leadership training, we were given nine hundred points then each discrepancy noted meant points subtracted from that score. A minimum score was required to graduate. That might be considered a bad illustration and it probably is, but I used it to make a point. We spent hours every evening shining boots, polishing floors and doing other chores getting ready. Is it possible that John is saying, "Get ready for the arrival of the master?"

Hope of Christ's coming motivates us to preparation. Many people say once you're saved you are always saved and therefore there is no need to expend effort toward "purifying yourself" for the coming day of the Lord. This text emphatically disputes that claim and offers this scripture as an indicator of true salvation: "Everyone who has this hope in him purifies himself, just as he is pure" (1 John 3:3). The doctrine of eternal security is scriptural. Jesus made it very clear in John chapter ten and other places in the bible. But it only applies to those who have been authentically saved.

A profession of faith is the beginning of preparation. Going forward during an invitation in a church doesn't save anyone. That privilege is afforded for those who have indeed believed in their heart that God raised Jesus from the dead after he had paid the price for their sins.

True salvation is only available to that individual who has unconditionally surrendered to Jesus and has experienced a change of heart, a change of mind and a change of behavior.

A Christian lifestyle is a part of preparation. While it is true that works doesn't save you and that you don't have to work to be saved, there is a theme running throughout the scriptures that what we do matters. There is the story of the land owner who gave three men a measure of talents.

"For everyone who has will be given more and he will have an abundance, whoever does not have, even what he has will be taken from him, and throw that worthless servant outside into the darkness where there will be weeping and gnashing of teeth." (156)

The footnote in the NIV says, "The main point of the parable, being ready for Christ's coming, involves more than playing it safe and doing little or nothing. It demands the kind of service that produces results." (157)

J. Vernon McGee puts it this way: "Brother, my question is not whether you are looking for the Lord to come, but how are you living down here? How you live down here determines whether or not you are really looking for the Lord to come." (158)

Grace is the beginning of a Christian lifestyle; faith produces works. I can already hear many who believe in "Grace plus nothing" mounting their argument. I do believe that grace plus nothing is the vehicle for salvation. But it is quite apparent throughout the New Testament that works are at the very least an indicator of whether an individual is authentically saved or not. It is impossible to ignore Ephesians 2:10: "For we are God's workmanship, created in Christ Jesus to do good works." I know I have made this point previously, but I must emphasize the point that if you are not involved in the works God has called you to perform, you are living in disobedience and therefore sin. I'm not the judge. I'm not qualified to be the judge, But Jesus is; and one day each of us will stand before him. Jesus tells us: "For the Son of man is going to come in His Father's glory with his angels and then he will reward each person according to what he has done" (Matthew 16:27).

Hope of Christ's coming leads to housecleaning. Make no mistake! If you are not saved, that is where you must start the purification process. John was talking to church members who were assumed to be Christians. So let's talk about 1 John 3:3, "Everyone who has this hope in him purifies himself, just as he (Jesus) is pure."

Have you ever had the privilege of expecting someone special to come see you or heard they were coming? Maybe a celebrity or a bride or a groom or even a long lost loved one. Remember how you scrubbed behind your ears and brushed your teeth? Or maybe you cleaned house until you almost wore out the carpet, or the floor. It is possible that John had something like that in mind when he said, "Everyone who has this hope."

There are those who are looking eagerly for the coming of Christ. I'm one of them. It is my hope that Jesus comes for me while I'm doing his work. Does that sound crazy? I'm sure it does to some, But I'm ready to go! Even so come Lord Jesus! Until he comes, however, I will continue the process of purification.

Hope of Christ's Coming leads to growth. What is John talking about when he says, "Everyone who has hope purifies himself."

Could it be that his point is supported by the apostle Peter when he tells us to, "Grow in grace and knowledge of our Lord and Savior Jesus Christ" (2 Peter 3:18). Or perhaps, observing the advice of the apostle Paul to, "Submit to one another out of reverence for Christ" (Ephesians 5:21). Or maybe even the commandment of our Lord Himself when he says, "A new command I give unto you: love one another. By this all men will know that you are my disciples if you have love for one another" (John 13:34–35). Perhaps the most pertinent one for us is found in 2 Timothy 2:15 NIV, "Do your best to present yourself to God as one approved, a workman who does not need to be ashamed." Or as found in the KJV, "Study to show thyself approved unto God, a workman that needeth not to be ashamed, rightly dividing the word of truth" (2 Timothy 2:15). I am relatively certain you can find some more or already know them.

Hope of Christ's coming leads to yieldedness. Although it is true the Holy Spirit is the purifying factor in our life, it is also true that he only works in us to the extent we are yielded to him and therefore it is important that we observe the advice of Paul, "Pray continually" (1 Thessalonians 4:17).

CHAPTER 15

Light on the Path of Righteousness Reveals Our Lifestyle as One of Translation or Transgression

1 John 3:4–7

While we were living at Fort Lee Virginia, I heard a very tragic story. I don't know if it's true or not because I wasn't a witness.

One afternoon I reported for work to find the place buzzing about one of the men having found a small child playing in a nest of baby rattlesnakes. He had rushed him to the hospital, but it was no use; the baby died because he had been bitten several times. Ignorance killed that baby. He had no idea that the creatures he was playing with were deadly. (159)

Some would like to use ignorance of God's law as an excuse to live in sin. To some extent, ignorance is a self-inflicted ailment; there are books beyond count; there are churches plentiful in almost every town, there are pastors/teachers on radio and TV and numerous other sources not mentioned that can dispel some ignorance.

For some, ignorance is a choice. A choice every one of us must make. It is a choice between translation and transgression. In Colossians 1:10–13 the apostle Paul informed the members of that congregation, "And we pray this in order that you may live a life worthy of the Lord and may please him in every way: bearing fruit in every good work, growing in knowledge of God for he has rescued you from the darkness and brought you into the kingdom of his dear Son." The King James Version has it written this way: "Who hath delivered us from darkness, and translated us into the Kingdom of his dear Son"

The Identification of Darkness as Sin was Discussed Previously

This will be an attempt to elaborate.

John makes a very clear case for the difference between trans-gression and translation. 1 John 3:4: "Everyone who sins breaks the law. In fact, sin is lawlessness."

Before we can understand *lawlessness*, we need to be aware of what John considered law to be in this context.

Baker's Dictionary of Theology defines law this way, "In a general sense the law is the whole of the revealed will of God. (160)

Guy H. King defines the law as, "God's will for his people." He says, the law, or "God's ideal," is sometimes, by some, deemed no longer relevant. (161)

I have heard individuals who were living in transgression of the law (sin) say: "We are no longer under the law, we live in the age of grace." It is my intent to outline the relevancy of the law and the reason for following it.

From the above definitions, we can say transgression is breaking the law of God

The law is always relevant over time. That relevance is pointed out in Matthew 5:18, where Jesus says, "For assuredly I say to you, till heaven and earth pass away, one jot or one tittle will by no means pass from the law until it is all fulfilled."

The law was relevant in Old Testament times. It would be no chore to convince most people who have read the Bible of the relevance of the law in Old Testament times. After all, the Ten Commandments were given to Moses in Exodus chapter twenty and recited in other places throughout the Old Testament. Leviticus is a book of laws so numerous we occasionally become confused when we try reading it.

The law was relevant in New Testament times. Jesus saw it as relevant in his time. "On one occasion an expert in the law stood up to test Jesus: "Teacher, he asked, 'What must I do to inherit eternal life? What is written in the Law?' He replied, 'How do you read it?'" (Luke 10:25–26).

The apostle Paul observed the law. It would be easy to view Paul's perspective as one who perceived the law as irrelevant to life, but that would be a misunderstanding of his position; this is confirmed by his statement in Acts 24:15: "But this I confess to you, that according to the way which they call a sect, so I worship the God of my fathers, believing all things which are written in the law and in the prophets."

The law is relevant to everyone today. It is relevant to non-Christians. It is relevant for non-Christians because it serves as a notice of condemnation for those without Christ. *Baker's Dictionary of Theology* points out that, "To fallen man, the law is an instrument for condemnation." (162)

Paul asks this question and answers it: "What shall we say then, is the law sin? Certainly not! On the contrary, I would not have known sin except through the law, for I would not have known covetousness unless the law had said, 'You shall not covet.' But sin, seizing the opportunity afforded by the commandment, produced in me every kind of covetous desire. For apart from the law, sin is dead. Once I was alive apart from law; but when commandment came, sin sprang to life and I died. I found that the very commandment that was intended to bring life, brought death. For sin, seizing the opportunity afforded by the commandment, deceived me, and through the commandment put me to death. Therefore, the law is holy and the commandment is holy and just and good." (163)

If the law only serves as a notice of condemnation, it would be a wicked and unjust thing. If that were true, how could we expect injustice from a just and loving God?

Because of his justice, he has made the law, not only to notify the unsaved of pending condemnation but to serve as a tutor pointing those who are under the threat of condemnation toward salvation. *Baker's Dictionary of Theology* tells us, "The law is a guide to show man the way to righteousness and points out Galatians 3:24, 'Therefore the law was our tutor to bring us to Christ that we might be justified by faith.'" (164)

Is this then a contradiction? Is John saying that those who perfectly keep the law can be saved? If we lived a perfect life and obeyed every law written, we still could not know salvation Romans 3:20 tells us, "Therefore by the deeds of the law, no flesh will be justified in his sight, for by the law is the knowledge of sin.

Salvation requires an intervention. 1 John 3:5 declares the availability of that event, "But you know that he appeared so that he might take away our sins."

If the wages of sin are death and all have sinned and come short of the glory of God, but you decide to change the way you live, "turn over a new leaf" so to speak, and start living in obedience to the law; that still wouldn't do away with sins of the past. Salvation is forgiveness of all sin for all time. That is the whole reason for Christ's coming. 1 John 3:8b tells us, "The reason the Son of God appeared was to destroy the devil's work."

Guy H. King points out that "Jesus's blood is the sovereign eraser of all our guilty stain." (165)

That's why 2 Corinthians 5:21 tells us, "God made him who knew no sin to be sin for us, so that in him we might become the righteousness of God." That's why Jesus hung on the cross in our place: "When you were dead in your sins and in the circumcision of your sinful nature, God made you alive with Christ. He forgave us all our sins. Having cancelled the written code, with its regulations, that was against us and that stood opposed to us. He took it away, nailing it to the cross." (166)

Why do you drive the speed limit? In a sociology class I was attending while working on my master's degree, I found myself in a debate with one of my professors over a traffic light. His contention was that the light was put there to control behavior. Mine was that it was there for safety. Of course, it is both; but to contend that it was only there to establish control, I believe, misses the greater point. That raises the question: Do you drive the speed limit because you are afraid of getting caught or do you drive the speed limit (if you do) because you recognize the need for safety? To put it in a more general sense: why do you obey the law?

The law is relevant to Christians. In view of Paul's description of grace as it is relevant to Christian behavior, why should Christians observe the law? In his epistles, Paul offers several scriptures that indicate our freedom from condemnation by the law. Romans 6:7 explains it like this: "Because anyone who has died has been freed from sin". Romans 6:14 could be interpreted as one of those suggestions of freedom from the law, "For sin shall not be your master, because you are not under law, but under grace." But that is not the intent of Paul at all. He declares in the very next verse: "What then? Shall we sin because we are not under the law but under grace? By no means! Don't you know that when you offer yourselves to someone to obey him as slaves, you are slaves to the one whom you obey—whether you are slaves to sin which leads to death, or obedience which leads to righteousness." (170)

So if the law is still relevant and if transgression of the law is sin, what's changed?

There is a sense in which one could say, "Translation is living above the law," but that perspective is clarified by John when he says, "No one who lives in him keeps on sinning" (1 John 3:6).

Ideally, Christians live above the law because we have been translated from the world of darkness into God's kingdom as indicated in Colossians 1:13.

That should be a reason for celebration. Free! Praise God! Free at last. The little song says, "Free from the fears of tomorrow, free from the guilt of the past. Freed from those shackles by his wonderful love; free, praise the Lord; free at last." (168)

"But if we're free from the price of sin, should we live as if sin no longer mattered?" Paul said this to that very pertinent question the Christians at Rome asked in chapter six. "What shall we say then? Shall we go on sinning so that grace may increase? By no means! We died to sin; how can we live in it any longer?" (Romans 6:2) The law is relevant to Christians but not in the same way as before conversion. We are informed in Romans 3: 30–31: "Since there is one God who will justify the circumcised by faith and the uncircumcised through faith, do we then make void the law through faith? Certainly not! On the contrary, we establish the law."

Christians are free from the power of sin. Not of ourselves; we have no power without the indwelling power of Jesus Christ to overcome sin and Satan; but that power over sin, at least in part, gives us a new motive for overcoming. That is the righteousness of Christ living in us and the love of God constantly before us.

Christians Receive Power to Resist Sin from the Indwelling Christ

Because the power to resist lies in Jesus Christ, that power is relevant to the level of our relationship to him.

Remember the story of Peter during the trial and crucifixion of Jesus? First, we find him following at a distance, In Matthew 26:58, the KJV tells us, "But Peter followed him afar off unto the High Priest's palace. The next time you read about him, he is sitting outside of where the trial is going on inside" (Matthew 26:69). "At last you find him mingling with the crowd" (Matthew 26:73).

Does that describe anybody you know? Power over sin is relevant. It is relevant to the extent of our involvement with Jesus.

Because Christians Have a New Father, a New Family, and a New Future, We Also Have a New Behavior

I am convinced that new behavior goes directly to motivation which leads to practice; this is clearly pointed out by John when he says: "No one who is born of God will continue to sin because God's seed remains in him." (1 John 3:9). It is because of that indwelling seed that Christians no longer practice sin.

All of us stumble from time to time, but because of the indwelling righteousness of our Savior and the intense love we have for God, we have a higher motive for observing the law than dos and don'ts. That is because we serve a new master.

There is no longer an obligation to the letter of the law because there has been an experience of rebirth and therefore Christians observe the spirit of the law. Since that is the case, is it right to say the written law has become an indication of obedience to God? We are told: "No one who lives in him, keeps on sinning; no one who continues to sin has either seen him or known him" (1 John 3:6).

John was writing to a group known as Gnostics who believed living a life of sin was okay because grace and the law were separate entities. I heard a pastor on TV this morning telling of a woman, to whom he was witnessing, say to him, "My life may be messed up but my heart's right." That is exactly what John is dealing with. He answered that attitude with this comment: "This is how we know who the children of God are and who the children of the devil are: anyone who does not do what is right is not a child of God; nor is anyone who does not love his brother."

What you do is what you believe. If we are living in obedience to the law as we know it, as Christians, the motivation for that behavior would not be fear, as in the past, but because of our love for God.

The price for sin has been paid. Jesus paid it for you on Calvary's cross. There is "Power in the Blood" "There is the power to save and the power to overcome sin. Do you have that power? There is a valid reason to change your behavior. What kind of life are you living? Can others see Jesus in you?

CHAPTER 16

Righteousness from the Inside Out
Lights the Path of Righteousness

1 John 3:7–10

Late in my teenage years, I worked as a bronc rider (horse trainer) for a rancher in western Oklahoma. On one occasion, he bought a herd of wild horses to be broken for sale to the army. Part of the preparation included trimming their manes and tails and combing the tangles out of their tails and trimming their hooves.

Needless to say, looking good wasn't enough. They had to be trained to ride, to rein, and to be gentle enough to be handled without too much danger because when the buyers came they would check not only for looks but for performance as well.

They would handle them from the ground, picking up each foot to inspect the hoof for damage or disease, pulling their tails, and rubbing them to feel for defects in their skin, etc. Then one person would ride each one while another watched how he travelled, that is, with his feet in a straight path and to check for a "broken wind." A problem that presents itself as a breathing problem and sometimes happens to horses who have been mishandled. (169)

Righteousness Is a Lifestyle

I hope you will pardon my analogy. It is not in any way to say we are horses, but it is a life experience told to make the point that righteousness is more than looking good. It also is relevant to performance. John informs us that: "Everyone who sins breaks the law; in fact, sin is lawlessness" (1 John 3:4).

1 John 3:7 emphasizes and defines lawlessness as doing that which is not right and says, "Dear children, do not let anyone lead you astray. He who does what is right is righteous."

Many are lead astray by false religions. Do you remember the hundreds who were lead to an Island by a man named Jones to be murdered or commit suicide? (170)

They were led astray by a feeling. An individual who had a certain amount of charisma, charm and Bible knowledge convinced them that conventional Christianity was not filling their needs. (170)

Perhaps you can remember the awful situation just outside of Waco, Texas, where a group of radically religious individuals set up a man to be a "prophet," built a compound and committed many religious atrocities in the name of God? Do you remember all the children and other innocent individuals who died in that situation? (170)

There are other organizations and "denominations" who lead individuals astray by mistranslation or misinterpretation of the Bible. John warns those to whom he was writing in John 3:7, "Do not let anyone lead you astray."

The best way to keep from being led astray is knowledge. I don't mean the knowledge about the Bible or about God from the overwhelming number of books available, although there are many very instructive ones on the market, but biblical knowledge, knowledge gleaned through constant prayer and Bible study.

There are activities available that will help avoid being led astray. Avoiding godless chatter is one way to avoid being led astray

Often, the "godless chatter" the apostle Paul speaks of in 2 Timothy 2:16 is one of the ways we are led astray. There he cautions us to "avoid godless chatter because those who indulge in it will become more and more ungodly."

When Paul told Timothy, "Do your best to present yourself to God as one approved, a workman that does not need to be ashamed and who correctly handles the word of truth" (2 Timothy 2:15). It was instructions for combating the heresy and false doctrines floating around him.

We mentioned Bible study above, but it is important to impress upon readers the importance of knowing false hood and dales teaching when it is presented. In 2 Timothy 2:15 KJV, the apostle Paul instructed Timothy: "Study to show thyself approved, a workman that needeth not to be ashamed."

The Bible is the inerrant inspired word of God. It is good for teaching and for learning the way of life and righteousness. It is the book that has been handed down for centuries to lead people to God and on the path of righteousness. If you don't understand what you read the first time, pray about it and read it again. In his time, God will reveal it to you.

Attend Bible-centered worship services. As you attend those Bible-centered worship services, listen to tested and qualified instruction. The writer of Hebrews offers this advice: "And let us not give up meeting together as some are in the habit of doing, but let us encourage one another—and so much more as you see the day approaching" (Hebrews 10:25).

John's purpose was to challenge Christians to righteous living and to point out how important it is in Christian life. He draws a very vivid and terse contrast when he declares: "He who does what is right is righteous, just as he is righteous" (1 John 3:7b).

Please allow me to repeat the definitions for religion and Christianity as I have been taught: "Religion is man seeking beyond himself for an answer to the unanswerable. Christianity, on the other hand, is God seeking man for his salvation." There may be other ways to say it but this is the central truth as taught in the Holy Scriptures. Although there are several things considered by those of worldly orientation more important than righteousness, they are not in themselves righteousness. Here consideration will be given to some of the more common ones.

Gnosticism is alive and well today. The Gnostics of John's day were extolling knowledge as the way of righteousness.

The *Holman Illustrated Bible Dictionary* tells us, "The term Gnosticism is derived from the Greek word Gnosis (knowledge) because secret knowledge was such a crucial doctrine in Gnosticism." (171)

Gnosticism is alive and well today. There are an overwhelming number of religious organizations and denominations who believe one should neither teach nor preach until they have attended their denominational seminary or college. That might have been the motivation for the rulers, elders, and teachers of the law to question Peter and John when they began to question them after the miracle they observed and recorded in the fourth chapter of Acts.

Christianity takes note of a right relationship with God. One very important consideration came into focus during the questioning of Peter and John by the Sanhedrin: "When they saw the courage of Peter and John and realized they were unschooled, ordinary men, they were astonished and they took note that these men had been with Jesus" (Acts 4:13).

The most important part of Peter and John's testimony was "That they had been with Jesus." That seemed to be most important to them and should be of most importance to us today. However, it should be pointed out here for those who are opposed to Christian education that Peter and John had spent three and a half years training with the Master Teacher, Jesus himself.

The question is not how many degrees you have from where but have you been with Jesus. Real righteousness is only available to those who have been with Jesus. You can have walls full of certificates and still be lost and without Christ.

Legalists say it is enough to behave a certain way. Another form of fabricated righteousness was practiced by the Judaizers of John's day. It dealt with behavior. There were some who dogged the paths of the apostles putting forth effort to convince those who were converted they were to do certain things. These individuals spent much time seeking a way to remove Paul from his perspective concerning salvation by grace. They even, on several occasions, tried to kill him. They had a superficial righteousness that was fake and unrealistic.

Christianity Says Real Righteousness Comes from the Inside Out

I have heard some—who should know better—say, "If you start behaving a certain way, eventually your perspective will change." Experience, training, and the scriptures teach the heart leads to righteousness. "For it is with your heart you are justified, and it is with your mouth that you confess and are saved" (Romans 10:10). Notice the heart came first. When I made my profession of faith, my heart had been changed. How about yours?

I know some "Judaizers." They practice a list of dos and don'ts and watch every movement of others to make sure the letter of their interpretation of morality is observed. These same people existed in Jesus's day.

Righteousness is not a list of dos and don'ts; it is a lifestyle of wills and won'ts. It is a lifestyle filled with a desire to be more like Jesus every day. It is a lifestyle that is formed from the inside out.

Some religions say it's about a beautiful ceremony. Have you ever heard someone say, "What a beautiful ceremony," or something similar?

A ceremony can be very moving and certainly has its place in worship. Throughout the scriptures, ceremony has been a part of history. Covenants between the patriarchs and the prophets and God are very much a part of God's relationship with his people. But if that's all there is, it's not nearly enough.

Baptism is a ceremony. If it is only a ceremony, it is blasphemy. Paul asked the church in Rome a very important question: "Or don't you know that all of us who were baptized into Christ Jesus were baptized into his death. We were therefore buried with him through baptism into death in order that, just as Christ was raised from the dead through the glory of the Father, we too may live a new life." (172)

This verse points out baptism as a ceremony that identifies Christians with our Savior, Jesus Christ. If, however, you have never experienced conversion or have not seriously and authentically accepted Christ as Lord and Savior, it then becomes another empty ceremony. Ceremony cannot save you! Baptism cannot make you righteous! Only Christ can do that. Righteousness—real righteousness, authentic righteousness—must come from the inside out. It must include a change of heart, a change of mind, and a change of behavior.

Self-righteousness can be a religion. In Romans, Paul talks about the form of righteousness that is probably most prevalent among religious people, including those who call themselves Christians; that is self-righteousness. He reveals this desire for the Jews of his day by saying: "Brothers, my heart's desire and prayer to God for the Israelites is that they may be saved for I can testify about them that they are very zealous for God, but their zeal is not based on knowledge. Since they did not know the righteousness that comes from God and sought to establish their own, they did not submit to God's righteousness." (173)

Those Who Are Self-Righteous Set Up Their Own Righteousness (Romans 10:3)

Self-righteousness is practiced by those who have never accepted Jesus as Lord and Savior and been converted but joined a church or a movement and began doing those things they believed righteous people would do. This is a description of the Pharisees. They rejected Christ as Lord and established their own style, or type, of religion.

They set themselves up as the epitome of righteousness because of pride and self-centeredness. They are the opposite of humility. They could not be taught because they are too full of themselves. I have a ridiculous but true observation: "You can't pour water in a full glass." Neither can you teach an individual who is convinced he knows everything. Humility and submission to the will of God is the key to salvation and to subsequent righteousness.

There is a righteousness that is real. It is the kind of righteousness that is not pretentious or superficial. It is a righteousness that is lived out in the world of daily living. In 1 Corinthians 1:30, the light found on the path of righteousness makes it very clear: "It is because of him that you are in Christ Jesus, who has become the wisdom from God—that is our righteousness, holiness and redemption." It seems to me the preceding verses make it very clear that real righteousness comes from God.

John MacArthur describes real righteousness this way, "The Holy Spirit implants in those he regenerates the principle of His divine life, which John sees as seed." (174)

In the story of the prodigal son, it was the father who welcomed him home. Granted, it was the son who came to the father, but it was the father who put a robe on him and made him welcome. It was the father who made the final choice. It is God who calls us to himself and dresses us with the robe of righteousness. Our robe isn't fit for the kingdom. Isaiah confesses in Isaiah 64:6, "Our righteous acts are as filthy rags."

Zechariah creates an excellent illustration as he paints this picture of salvation: "Joshua appears as one polluted but is purified; for he represents the Israel of God, who are all as an unclean thing, till they are washed and sanctified in the name of the Lord Jesus and by the Spirit of our God."

"Now Joshua was clothed with filthy garments, and stood before an angel and he answered and spoke unto those that stood before him, saying, 'Take away the filthy garments from him.' And unto him he said, 'Behold I have caused thine iniquity to pass from thee, and I will clothe thee with a change of raiment.' And I said, 'Let them set a fair mitre on his head.' So they set a mitre upon his head, and clothed him with garments." (175)

We are metaphorically identified with this even in Zechariah. We are the one standing before the throne clothed in the filth of sin and shame. It is God who provides the robe of righteousness and washes us in the blood of his son, Jesus Christ.

Did the prodigal son clean himself up on the way home? The story stands. He was received by the father with all his guilt and with all his filth and with the smell of a hog pen all over him then he was cleaned up and offered a new robe and a ring and the fatted calf. If we consider righteousness as conditional we have missed the omniscient power of an all-powerful, all-seeing God. Look again at 1 John 3:1: "How great is the love the Father has lavished on us that we should be called the children of God." Remember the vehicle for salvation: "For it is by grace (undeserved mercy) you have been saved, through faith—and that not from yourselves, it is the gift of God—not by works, so that no one can boast." (Ephesians 2:8)

Matthew Henry tells us, "Thus does the grace of God provide for true penitents. First, the righteousness of Jesus Christ is the robe, that principle robe, with which they are clothed; they that put on the Lord Jesus Christ are clothed with that Sun. The robe of righteousness is the garment of salvation." (176)

If righteousness is a gift from God, then how can 1 John 3:8 even be relevant?

Matthew Henry makes a valid point when he uses the term "true penitents." (177) Grace is available but grace is not always received. Because there is another seed planted in the heart of some. In 1 John 3:8, he makes the statement: "He who does what is sinful is of the devil, because the devil has been sinning from the beginning."

John MacArthur makes the valid point that, "All unsaved sinners are in a sense the devil's children."

Jesus told the Pharisees, "You belong to your father the devil, and you want to carry out the desires of your father. He was a murderer from the beginning and has never stood by the truth, since there is no truth in him." Whenever he tells a lie he speaks in character, for he is a liar and the father of lies. (178)

It Is Impossible to Please God If You Are Unsaved

It is impossible to live righteously without having been born again, "Because the carnal mind is enmity against God: for it is not

146

subject to the law of God neither indeed can be. So then they that are in the flesh cannot please God" (Romans 8:7–8).

Evidence of the fatherhood of Satan is making the claim to righteousness then denying its existence by living a lifestyle that does not glorify God.

The consequences of such a lifestyle are exposed with great clarity in the New Testament. Paul pointed that out to the church in Corinth with this remark: "Do you not know that the wicked will not inherit the kingdom of God? Do not be deceived; Neither the sexually immoral nor idolaters nor adulterers nor male prostitutes nor homosexual offenders nor thieves nor the greedy nor drunkards nor swindlers will inherit the kingdom of God and that is what some of you were, but you were washed, you were sanctified, you were justified (made righteous) in the name of the Lord Jesus Christ and by the Spirit of our God." (179)

Paul also very graphically pointed out to the church at Corinth the change in their life brought about by allowing Christ to come into their lives and submitting to his Lordship. It is of utmost importance to make Christ Lord of our life because if he is not Lord, he cannot be Savior.

It is he who makes us righteous as we submit to him from the inside out. That is why John said: "No one who is born of God will continue to sin, because God's seed remains in him; he cannot go on sinning because he has been born of God" (1 John 3:9).

There seems to be some confusion and some misinformation about who is really saved and who is not. There is a short simple answer that is pointed out clearly in Romans 3:7–10, "Anyone who does not do what is right is not a child of God."

If righteousness is not evident in our lifestyle, how is it possible to claim it?

CHAPTER 17

Light on the Path of Righteousness
Reveals Confirmation by Love

1 John 3:11–8

John considered love as evidence of salvation to such an extent that he pointed it out again and again. He informs us that, "This is the message you heard from the beginning: we should love one another" (1 John 3:11).

John MacArthur points out that, "God not only commands those who are in Christ to show love (cf. John 15:12; I Peter 4:8), He also enables them to obey that mandate, granting them the capacity to do what He requires." (180)

It is a great thing to attend church and sing praise songs and fellowship with other church members and that is certainly an important part of Christianity, but being a Christian is sharing and showing love for God and those around us. Real love is revealed by the way we behave toward those who visit our church and with whom we associate in the world where we are surrounded by the reality of sin, temptation, and challenges to our faith.

Love of God is revealed not only in the good times previously mentioned; it is revealed by our attitude toward to him in times of testing.

When Peter and John were tested, they had a response that everyone should be able to answer correctly. Their response to those who would be their persecutors was, "Judge for yourselves whether it is right in God's sight to obey you rather than God" (Acts 4:19).

The subject of loving obedience is not one to be taken lightly. Jesus said, "Not everyone who says to me Lord, Lord, will enter the kingdom of heaven but only he who does the will of my Father who is in heaven" (Matthew 7:21).

Why do you think a discussion of obedience is relevant here? Because obedience is a revelation of our love; Jesus said, "If you love me, you will obey what I command" (John 14:15).

Love reveals the difference between those who are lost and those who are saved. John pointed out that contrast in 1 John 3:10b, "Anyone who does not do right is not a child of God; nor is anyone who does not love his brother."

Love is confirmed by loyalty. It is different than obedience. While obedience is following the desires and the example of Jesus, loyalty is living a life that reflects Christianity in times of difficulty as well as regular times. John forewarned his readers, "Do not be surprised, my brothers, if the world hates you" (1 John 3:13).

John MacArthur states, "Rather than being shocked by the world's opposition, believers should instead expect it. (cf. Acts 14:22; 2 Timothy 3:12; 2 Peter 4:12), because the world has nothing in common with the kingdom of God." (181)

When John and Peter stood before their persecutors in Acts 4:19, they demonstrated their loyalty. When Stephen testified before they stoned him in Acts chapters six and seven, he showed his loyalty.

While stationed in Germany, in addition to my military duty, I was involved in starting a church about forty miles from my duty station and became the pastor. During that time, I was also promoted by the army.

Upon having received the orders and attending an in ranks ceremony, I was called in to see the first sergeant. "Stafford," he said, "tonight we are going to wet down your stripes at the NCO club. You will be there."

"Wetting down my stripes" meant everybody was going to celebrate the promotion by getting drunk and being involved in an obscene party.

My response was "I can't make it because I don't drink." He knew why and he knew I was pastor of a church.

"You will make it, or I will have your stripes."

"First Sergeant, you didn't give me my stripes and you can't take them," I informed him, with some trepidation.

I didn't go, and by standing up for my faith, I earned the respect of a very tough first sergeant. We later became friends. (182)

Some have said, "The right thing to do would have been to go and drink a soft drink instead of alcohol." When you begin to compromise with sin, you will not only compromise the opinion of others about you; you will be subjecting yourself to temptation that could and should be avoided.

Today there is an increasing resistance to Christianity. There are more and more opportunities to show loyalty. The present administration is mounting a subtle attack even now upon our religious right to be free from government control. It's time to ask yourself, "When the time comes, will I be found faithful?"

Paul warned the church at Ephesus of the battle they were in and that battle still goes on today. It isn't a physical battle—that would be a lot easier for some of us—but he makes it very clear that it's a spiritual one: "For our struggle is not against flesh and blood, but against rulers, against the authorities, against the powers of this dark world and against the spiritual forces of evil in heavenly realms" (Ephesians 6:12).

The answer to their dilemma, and to ours, is found in the preceding verse: "Finally be strong in the Lord and in his mighty power. Put on the whole armor of God so that you can take your stand against the devil's schemes" (Ephesians 6:10–11 KJV).

It is one thing to sing, "O How I Love Jesus," and quite another to show it in the world where wickedness and rebellion are to be found virtually everywhere. Jesus commanded our loyalty when he said, "My command is this: love each other as I have loved you. Greater love has no one than this; that he lay down his life for his friends" (John 15:12–13). And it is even more emphatically expressed in Mark 12:30: "Love the Lord your God with all your heart and with all your soul and with all your mind and with all your strength."

Love is considered a birthmark that confirms the reality of salvation. Guy H. King says, "Here is one mark by which you may test yourself. 1 John 3:14 points out that, 'We know we have passed from death to life, because we love our brothers.' This is not the cause of translation, but the evidence of it." (183)

Harold T. Bryson calls love "the birthmark of believers." In his book entitled *Increasing the Joy*, he makes this very valid statement: "The believers' spiritual birthmark is a love for one another." (184)

That message of love had been proclaimed by John's and his fellow messengers from the beginning of their ministry with Jesus. It was pointed out by Jesus himself, not only in word but by the miracles and acts of compassion he performed. It is the same message throughout the New Testament, and it is just as relevant today.

We cannot start a conversation concerning love without discussing the love God expressed for us when he gave his only begotten Son for us on Calvary. Paul says in Ephesians 2:4–5, "But because of his great love for us, God who is rich in mercy, made us alive with Christ even when we were dead in transgression—it is by grace you are saved." Love is action, and the action of Jesus Christ on the cross was an expression of the love God has for us.

Christians are channels of God's love. J. Vernon McGee says, "Our tongue is very good at running ahead of our feet, but true Christianity, the real article, is a matter of the heart and not of the head or tongue." (185)

John confirms his statement and offers further evidence of authentic salvation: "This is how we know what love is: Jesus laid down his life for us, and we ought to lay down our lives for our brothers." (1 John 3:16).

Although there is a possibility that one might be required to give one's life for the faith, John is pointing out here the need for Christians to give their lives to their faith. This is in line with the teachings of Paul who said in Romans 12:1, "Therefore I urge you, brothers, in view of God's mercy, to offer your bodies as living sacrifices, holy and pleasing to God—this is your spiritual worship."

The KJV uses the term here "reasonable service" for spiritual worship.

Illness in the family prompted me to resign my last church about one hundred eighty miles from my permanent residence and move back home to take care of one of my daughters. That experience produced an excellent demonstration, in my view, of what the apostle Paul meant in a previously-mentioned scripture.

One of the members of that church helped us clean the place where we were living, and drove one of my vehicles the one hundred eighty miles home for me because my wife cannot drive because of arthritis, without one drop of reimbursement for the time he lost and the money he spent. (186)

To me, that is a testimony of love. He has a lifestyle of helping others either with money or with effort. To me he is the epitome of presentation of our bodies as a living sacrifice and a demonstration of the love John was talking about.

Although many of us could list experiences like the one I mentioned above, laying your life down for a friend goes much farther than that sometimes; it also includes daily living, including everyday happenings as we live with and among others.

Courtesy and benevolence sometimes come in little things one does or says like an expression of concern or an act of assistance or just plain friendliness. I am constantly appalled by an apparent lack those expressions of love by many in the marketplace and in the church.

Lack of concern for others can lead to isolation and from there to fear of association with others leading to an opening for Satan to influence our life.

For Satan to conquer our heart, he doesn't need to physically overcome us. He simply needs to establish fear in our heart. Actual statistics reveal there is only a very small number of people, comparatively speaking, that even witness the things we see on TV, much less experience them. Paul had an answer for this problem for Christians in his letter to Timothy: "For God hath not given us the spirit of fear; but of power, and of love, and of a sound mind" (2 Timothy 1:7).

I have been involved in the starting of several new churches in different areas, including one in Germany. I am always amazed when interest is shown to places in other lands while a local work goes begging. I'm not complaining. I'm merely making the point that missions are as much boots on the ground as they are checks overseas. Hahn Baptist Church, the one I was involved with in Germany, grew from an attendance of thirty-six in a soldier's living room to a regular attendance of one hundred eighty-three in eighteen months because the members were involved in outreach benevolence and loving others. It should be pointed out here that I couldn't visit on base without invitation; therefore, we must credit the work to the members of that congregation with any results and give God the glory.

Jesus made a very pertinent comment to the Pharisees of his day: "Woe to you teachers of the law and Pharisees, you hypocrites! You give a tenth of your spices—mint, dill, and cumin. But you have neglected the more important matters of the law—justice, mercy, and faithfulness. You should have practiced the latter without neglecting the former" (Matthew 23:23). Notice he did not make it a matter of choice: giving or helping but both giving and helping.

Love is expressed through giving. For most of us, it isn't that difficult to write a check. The act of participating in the work of foreign missions is a romantic endeavor. It is an opportunity for rejoicing for most givers, when some amount sent overseas somewhere is announced, and it should be. Although the real joy in my life is when I personally witness an individual accepting Jesus as Lord and Savior, since my personal testimony is very limited I find it appropriate to give to missions at home and abroad.

For many Christians, tithing is ten percent because we have been taught that is the definition of "a tenth," but I would like to present another possibility. Real Christian tithing is thirty percent. Based on Jesus's statement above, it includes ten percent of your time, ten percent of your talent, and ten percent of your finances. If you do that, you have done that which is pleasing to the Lord and will promote loving growth in the church.

I know of one church where they give their proud ten percent to the cooperative program. They give to state missions and support a children's home with their money, but they had no program for local benevolence and one of the members offered adamant and determined resistance to initiating a local plan. On at least two occasions he resisted helping those who sought help from the church, this is the subject addressed by John when he says: "Dear children, let us not love with words or tongue but with actions and in truth" (1 John 3:18)

Love is expressed by personal outreach. Real love—Christian love—is expressed by going in to the highways and byways, physically getting involved in the life of someone who needs help.

Many of our churches offer programs to help those in physical, medical, or psychological need as an expression of Christian love.

That is the kind of involvement John was talking about in the verse quoted above. The Good Samaritan could have laid some money on the chest of the wounded man he encountered as recorded in Luke 10:30–35, but he became personally involved.

The scriptures tell us, "He went to him and bandaged his wounds, pouring on oil and wine, then he put the man on his own donkey, took him to an inn and took care of him" (Luke 10:34). That is what John is encouraging his readers to do. Become involved. You may never find a wounded individual lying beside the road, but the world is full of those who need a kind word or a helping hand. Authentic Christian love means getting involved. How involved are you?

CHAPTER 18

Light on the Path of Righteousness Reveals How You Can Know You Are Saved

1 John 3:19–24

In a small paperback book written by a Catholic priest named David Knight, I found this beautiful illustration which he credited to Booker T. Washington: "Booker T. Washington tells of a ship becalmed off the South American coast when sails were still more common than steam. Crew members were starting to die of thirst when a steamship hove in sight. 'Send us water,' they signaled. The steamship signaled back, 'Send down your bucket where you are,' the story goes. 'It is fresh water we need. Send us drinking water.' Still the steamship signaled back, 'Send down your bucket where you are.'

"When the crew of the sailing vessel finally did lower their bucket into the ocean, it came up filled with fresh, not salt, water. The fresh water of the Amazon river is carried 50 miles out to sea when it pours out of its mouth on the coast of Brazil—or so the story goes."

He goes on to say, "Whether the Amazon River really does this, I don't know, but the key line of this story could serve as the guiding principle of lay spirituality: send down your bucket." (187)

Let down your bucket, put your trust to the test. In 1 John 3:19–24, John invites us to let down our bucket. He makes this state-

155

ment in verse 19, "This then is how we know that we belong to the truth."

Guy H. King makes this comment about 1 John 3:19–24, "The phrase apparently connects with what has just been said, in the previous verses, and refers to the possession and practice of a loving Christian spirit.

"If we believe the evidence, walk in the light, walk as Jesus walked, refuse the forbidden love of the world, and sincerely love God and others in an active and constructive way then we can be assured, we belong to the truth." (188)

No! It is not the letter of the law! It is the natural behavior of an individual who has undergone a conversion experience and has become a "new creation in Christ Jesus." That experience reveals the lack of sufficiency and creates a strong dependency on God. The apostle Paul expresses it like this: "Not that we are sufficient of ourselves to think of anything as being from ourselves, but our sufficiency is from God, who also made us sufficient as ministers of the new covenant, not of the letter (the Ten Commandments) but of the Spirit; for the letter kills but the Spirit gives life." (189)

He says elsewhere, "By the law no one can be saved." It's really righteousness from the inside out. It is a lifestyle generated by the indwelling of a loving Savior. John MacArthur quotes a phrase written by Jonathan Edwards and says: "Edwards in 1746 wrote his classic book, *A Treatise Concerning Religious Affections.* This monumental work argues that the most accurate proof of salvation is in the presence in one's life of holy, religious affections—a zealous and biblical inclination toward righteousness, evidenced by practical good works." (190)

We can know we are saved when we realize God is greater than our feelings. I can personally testify that in my life a lot of things I should have done were not, and that a lot of things were done that shouldn't have been done. There are times when I start thinking about all the failures and all the mistakes and all the sin in my life, and I get the "Woe-Is-Me Itis." Isaiah said, "Woe is me for I am undone" (Isaiah 6:5).

Do you ever feel undone? John must have expected us to have that experience, and perhaps had been there himself. He said, "This is how we know we belong to the truth, and how we set our hearts at rest in his presence." (1 John 3:19) He continued the thought by elaborating on his statement: "If our hearts condemn us, God is greater than our hearts, and he knows everything" (1 John 3:20).

I can question my salvation, but God remembers that little tow-headed boy who climbed in the back of Violet Hobb's pickup and went to meet Jesus.

He remembers those days when I was in innocent darkness and oblivion, and he sent a neighbor lady to take me to him. "God is greater than our hearts, because he knows everything." I am reminded of the song, "He Was There All the Time."

Can you understand the plight of the sailors mentioned at the beginning of this chapter? They were literally dying of thirst and, to their knowledge, no good water was available.

John says, "Let down your bucket." This is how we set our hearts at rest in his presence whenever our hearts condemn us, "For God is greater than our hearts."

There are those who say this verse speaks of even greater condemnation. Matthew Henry says, "If conscience condemns us, God does so too—God is a greater witness than our conscience, and knoweth more against us than our conscience does." (191) But that is looking at God as a witness for the prosecution. Why would he send his only begotten Son to save me then condemn me for not following the law?

The Arminian position teaches that salvation is conditional. They believe Christians can lose their salvation, and do, through unrepented sin, denial, disbelief or some other contrived discrepancy. But Paul says it is by grace we are saved, not of ourselves; he says in Romans 5:10, "For if, when we were God's enemies, we were reconciled to him through the death of his Son, how much more, having been reconciled, shall we be saved through his life." In Romans 5:6 of the same chapter, he says, "You see, at just the right time, when we were still powerless, Christ died for the ungodly."

Jesus says in John 10: 28, "I give them eternal life, and they shall not perish, no one can snatch them out of my hand."

We can know we are saved when we have a sincere desire to follow Jesus. The point should be made here that authentic salvation is not just an event in life. Jesus makes it very clear that salvation is an event, an ongoing experience, and an ultimate experience: He describes authentic Christians by declaring: "My sheep listen to my voice; I know them and they follow me and I give them eternal life" (John 10: 27).

Thus, the biblical position contradicts the perspective of "free grace," which teaches that "justified people" are saved forever regardless of their lifestyle; even if they only follow Christ's teaching for a little while. This position holds the belief that an individual is saved once a decision is made to follow Christ, no matter whether he or she overtly denies Christ or merely lives the rest of his or her life uninterested in matters honoring the Lord. Behavior of the many professors who do not live lives that reflect Christ indicates this as a prevalent perspective today.

We can know we are saved when we have a sincere love for others. John makes this point in several places, having a sincere love for others is a way of knowing if we are saved. One such statement is: "We know that we have passed from death to life, because we love our brothers; anyone who does not love remains in death" (1 John 3:14).

This is not a love that can be forced or faked. It is not a feeling conjured up because it is a requirement for salvation. It is not a requirement so much as it is a gift that is part of the package.

Christians do not love each other because of obedience but because they have undergone a significant change: It is called a new nature Paul describes that transformation like this: "Therefore, if anyone is in Christ, he is a new creation; the old has gone the new has come! All this is from God who has reconciled us to himself through Christ and gave us the ministry of reconciliation." (192)

The letter of 1 John is about authenticity. Jesus phrased it like this: "By their fruit you will recognize them, do people pick grapes from thorn bushes or figs from thistles?" (Matthew 7:16).

The fruit is a testimony about the root. The apostle Paul repeats the analogy used by Jesus and says: "But the fruit of the spirit is love, joy, peace, patience, kindness, goodness, faithfulness, gentleness, and self -control. Against such things there is no law. Those who belong to Christ Jesus have crucified the sinful nature with its passions and desires." (193)

To understand the difference between forced obedience and the gift of obedience we must make special note of the beginning of Galatians 5:22. That same fruit is pointed out by John as evidence of conversion: "Those who obey his commands live in him, and he in them. And this is how we know that he lives in us. We know it by the Spirit he gave us" (1 John 3:24).

John MacArthur says: "In contrast to the Arminianism and free life Grace, which either make assurance impossible to keep or provide the wrong criteria for sustaining it. John wrote this epistle so that those who believe in the name of the Son of God may know that (they) have salvation." (194)

It must be said here that not everyone and probably not anyone lives the life described by Paul, John, and Jesus one hundred percent of the time to the maximum extent possible but there is a genuine effort to live up to the standard set by those great men.

Knowing in your heart you are free from condemnation is proof of salvation. Can you imagine the relief of those sailors mentioned earlier who were stranded and becalmed on the sea when they tasted that fresh water? John gives that same picture to every Christian who has the blessed assurance of salvation many times over. He offers these words of comfort, "Dear friends, if our hearts do not condemn us, we have confidence before God" (1 John 3:21).

In the fourth chapter of John, the woman at the well found living water, when she believed the words of Jesus. That same living water is available to you and me as we believe the words of the Bible and learn to trust his instruction. The old hymn says, "Trust me try me prove me and I will pour out a blessing on you." In other words, "Let your bucket down." Living water is available.

We can know we are saved by an active faith in Jesus as Savior. Someone has said, "Faith is walking to the edge of light and taking one more step." Mature faith is taking that step while resting in the assurance that God will take care of everything. For many, it's hard to believe or understand the message and the meaning of Romans 8:28, but it has been a source of comfort for me many times. There, the apostle Paul assures us with these words. "And we know that in all things God works for the good of those who love him, who have been called according to his purpose."

There are occasions where that seems questionable; even times when it appears untrue due to our narrow understanding, but if we are going to believe the Bible is the inerrant, infallible Word of God, we must accept Romans 8:28 as a concrete promise.

Although I'm relatively sure it is not recommended today, one of the cures used by my parents in the backwoods of Oklahoma for a sore throat when I was a child was "coal oil and sugar." I hated that stuff. It refused to be swallowed without coaxing, coercion, and liquid help; but it usually cured a sore throat—or so Mama said. Likewise, there are things that happen in our present lives that aren't all that pleasant but are good for us. (196)

The key consideration here is our obedience and faith. John informs us, "This is his command: to believe in the name of his Son, Jesus Christ, and to love one another as he commanded us" (1 John 3:23).

Many individuals pray in a distorted or haphazard way. The request is often delivered in a very selfish form one example seems to imply, "Not thy will but mine be done." Jesus prayed in the garden, "Yet not as I will, but as you will" (Matthew 26:39). That statement indicates humility, submission, and obedience; that is the only way to come to God.

John points out evidence of authenticity once again in 1 John 3:24 when he informs his readers: "Those who obey his commands live in him, and he in them." This and previous statements destroy the position that an individual can make a "profession of faith" then go on living a life filled with behavior that denies Christ and actually be a partaker of eternal security.

For one to possess everlasting life he or she must first have been a partaker of the rebirth that is a gift from God to those who authentically believe and are changed. John says: "We know it by the Spirit he gave us."

Are you a vessel for the Holy Spirit God has given to every authentic Christian? Is it reflected in your lifestyle? If it isn't, perhaps you need to repent of your sins and ask Christ to really come into your life to be your Lord and Savior.

CHAPTER 19

Light on the Path of Righteousness Can Be Used for Testing the Spirits

1 John 4:1–6

"The spirit just told me the men should gather in one of the back rooms to talk with the pastor." These were the words of a man who claimed to be Baptist and was recognized as a leader in a certain Baptist church but followed the doctrine of a "Holiness Non-Denominational" organization. He had been in that Baptist church for several years, and the pastors had allowed him to propagate his doctrine without correction. Consequently, he was deeply entrenched.

It isn't a question of whether Baptists are any better or worse than others. It's a question of being what you say you are. This man was claiming one thing while believing another. To me, that is hypocrisy, or worse. It is lying to further your own agenda or for self-aggrandizement. That could come under the description of Antichrist. The Gnostics were wrong, but for the most part, they apparently were sincere in their beliefs.

All the men gathered in a room as per the "revelation" of this individual who presented himself publicly as a Baptist while practicing the doctrine of another denomination where he proceeded to "straighten out" the new pastor. This went on for some time until one of the other church leaders brought it to an end.

His "spiritual revelations" continued to be one of his frequent claims as time went forward, with most of them aimed at the pastor, and all of them detrimental to the health of the church.

He had a practice of gathering the men in a little group in the churchyard to discuss the many alleged faults and shortcomings of the pastor out of his hearing range. One such Sunday morning, the pastor walked in on their little conference. His words were "Pastor, you are not supposed to be here."

Because of the length of time he had been practicing his deceit, and because of his "charisma," that pastor was unable to minister to that congregation and finally resigned to allow someone else the opportunity for ministry.

This is an example that should cause all Christians to heed the advice of John, "Dear friends, do not believe every spirit, but test the spirits to see whether they are of God" (1 John 4:1).

As we have journeyed through this letter from John, we have exposed certain elements, perspectives and positions held by a group labeled "Gnostics." Chapter four, verses one through six of 1 John contain instruction concerning the recognition of authenticity among Christians as opposed to the manufactured doctrine of the Gnostics.

It Is Difficult to Recognize Some Who Have the Spirit of Antichrist

Remember, John wrote this letter to combat the doctrine of the Gnostics in his time. Donald Guthrie's work concerning New Testament theology tells us, "There appear to be some who were calling themselves apostles at Corinth, whose views Paul found it necessary to combat. In 2 Corinthians 11:13, Paul calls them 'false prophets' who disguised themselves as 'apostles of Christ.'" (196)

In the NIV Student Bible marginal notes, we find this explanation of the Gnostic doctrine, and it begins with asking this question:

"Could God have a body? Gnostics balked at the Christian concept of God becoming human. Because they believed a physical body was intrinsically evil, they denied that a pure God could take a body . . ." (197)

"The apostle John debated in person with Gnostics of his day, and he had Gnostic thinking in mind when he wrote this letter. The first sentence expressly states that the author has seen, heard and touched Jesus—implying that he could not have been a phantom or pure spirit."

The first place one should turn to test spiritual authenticity or the lack of it is God's Holy Word, the Bible. Jesus said, "Search the Scriptures for in them you think you have eternal life."

It has never been more important to search the scriptures than it is today. In 1 John 4:1b, John says, "Test the spirits to see whether they are from God." Even today some who are claiming to be "people of the book" have begun to distort the reading of the Bible by words or phrases out of context or ignoring Biblical teaching completely.

Doctrinal authenticity must be supported by the Bible. There are those, among us whom, I sadly confess, some of my own family are numbered, who claim exclusive authenticity yet ignore several biblical truths found in the scripture.

John makes it very clear that one of the tests for authenticity is confession that Jesus came in the flesh, died for our sins, was resurrected from the grave, ascended into heaven and will return for us. The following statement appears in Barnes Notes: "If there were no real sufferings; there were no shedding of blood; there was no death on the cross; then of course there was no atonement for sin." (198)

The writer of Hebrews states: "Without the shedding of blood there is no forgiveness" (Hebrews 9:22b).

Those who believe the "church" is able to save the lost have forgotten Jesus's words in John 14:6, "Jesus answered, 'I am the way the truth and the life. No one comes to the Father except through me.'"

Those who claim baptism as a path to salvation and consequently believe in baptism of babies have ignored the scripture that teaches the necessity of confession. Paul outlines the path to salvation this way, "If you confess with your mouth, 'Jesus is Lord,' and believe in your heart that God raised him from the dead, you will be saved" (Romans 10:9).

Those who disclaim the deity of Christ have ignored the prophecy of Isaiah that declares the coming of Christ in these words: "Therefore the Lord himself will give you a sign. The virgin will be with child and will give birth to a son, and will call him Immanuel" (Isaiah 7:14).

The *Baker's Dictionary of Theology* translates the word *Immanuel* as a transliterated Hebrew name meaning "God with us" and further states that it is found not only in Isaiah 7:14, but in Isaiah 8:8, 10 and Matthew 1:23. (199)

There is a myriad of other scriptures that confirm the deity and the purpose and position of Christ concerning his existence and his deity.

The purpose for his coming is revealed in Luke 19:10, "The Son of Man came to seek and to save what was lost." Paul points out that his position while he was here in the flesh was that of a suffering servant and finally a sacrificial lamb: "Who being in very nature God, did not consider equality with God something to be grasped, but made himself nothing, taking the form of a servant, being made in human likeness, and being found in appearance as a man, he humbled himself and became obedient unto death—and even death on a cross." (200)

All the books of the New Testament confirm, in one way or another, the fact that Jesus came in the flesh, dwelt among us, and died in our place on the cross for our sins.

There are so many other strange and unscriptural practices and doctrines, it would take another book to reveal them; consequently, the best advice available is to "test" them by the measurement of the Holy Scriptures.

"This is how you can recognize the Spirit of God: Every spirit that acknowledges that Jesus Christ has come in the flesh is from God but every spirit that does not acknowledge Jesus is not of God." (201)

I would like to ask you: do you acknowledge Jesus Christ as the one who came in the flesh, died a literal death on the cross and rose from the grave the third day? If not I pray that some of the information printed here will help you come to that conclusion.

Christians Have a Special Spirit

John points out a stark difference between the saved and unsaved. He informs the Parthian churches to whom he was writing, "You, dear children, are from God" (1 John 4:4a). Before they were saved, however, their father was the devil; Jesus describes them as such and points out their relationship to the devil in John 8:44: "You belong to your father, the devil, and you want to carry out your father's desire."

Some would respond with the statement that the people Jesus was talking to were the Pharisees, and that is true, but I see people almost every day who fit the description of the Pharisees. They too claim Christianity but live lives of sin and deceit. May I remind you of a quote from Jesus we have used previously when he said, "By their fruits you shall know them."

Those who lust after things of the world and practice the ways of the world are not saved and, therefore, can properly be considered children of Satan. This can be substantiated by the words of Paul when he informs us, "The sinful mind is hostile to God. It does not submit to God's law, nor can it do so" (Romans 8:7).

Those who are controlled by the sinful nature cannot please God because they are ignorant of the ways of righteousness.

Christians seek after righteousness. Righteousness is defined by *Unger's Bible Dictionary* as: "Purity of heart and rectitude of life; the being and doing right." (202)

Donald Guthrie refers to Habakkuk 2:4 as a demonstration of righteousness, "The righteous will live by his faith," then goes on to explain it from Paul's perspective.

He further states, "The righteous man is one who is accepted by God, but Paul extends his own understanding of it to see its fullest expression in personal faith in Jesus Christ. When someone exercises such faith, he becomes righteous in God's sight." (203)

That certainly would coincide with the instruction of Christ himself. In Matthew 5:6, he informs his listeners: "Blessed are those who hunger and thirst for righteousness for they will be filled." The apostle Paul described the ultimate reward of those who are righteous: "For the Lord, himself will come down from heaven, with a loud command, with the voice of the archangel and with the trumpet call of God, and the dead in Christ will rise first. After that, we who are still alive and are left will be caught up together with them in the air. And so, we will be with the Lord forever." (204)

Christians Love Others

Love is a theme we have already discussed while exploring 1 John. It is a subject we will discuss even more as we move forward in our discussion. The Bible expounds a great deal on this subject and that apparently emphasizes the importance of it. If you recall, John has already informed us in 1 John 3:14, "Anyone who does not love remains in death."

The apostle Paul thought love was so important, he dedicated a whole chapter in 1 Corinthians 13 and described it as more important than anything else one could do.

"If I speak in the tongue of men and of angels, but have not love, I am only a sounding gong or a clanging cymbal. If I have the gift of prophecy and can fathom all mysteries and all knowledge, and I have faith that can move mountains, but have not love, I am nothing. If I give all I possess to the poor and surrender my body to the flames but have not love, I gain nothing." (205)

Love is the paramount evidence of conversion. There are those even today who call themselves Christian while they spitefully use others and take advantage by lying and cheating. Would you call this behavior an expression of Christian love?

Decide for yourself as you read God's word. Are individuals who behave like that really saved? How about you? How do you express your love for others? Can others see Jesus in you? If they can't maybe he really isn't there. I'm not qualified to judge, but Jesus is, and the Bible says each of us will someday give account to him for our life here on earth.

Christians recognize the greatness of God. Christians see God as the creator of the universe. They accept Genesis 1:1 as true when it states, "In the beginning God created the heavens and the earth." Christians recognize him as the God of all comfort. Paul made this strong statement: "Praise be to the God and Father of our Lord Jesus Christ, the Father of compassion and the God of all comfort" (2 Corinthians 1:3). We could appropriately add, "And the Father of all who accept his Son as Lord and Savior."

Paul informs the church in Rome: "So then, He is Father of all who believe and have not been circumcised, in order that righteousness might be credited to them" And he is also the father of the circumcised who not only are circumcised but who also walk in the footsteps of the faith that our father Abraham had before he was circumcised." (206)

Christians Have Special Privileges

There is the privilege of becoming a co-heir with Christ in the Kingdom of God. The family relationship of Christians is manifested in certain privileges and behaviors. One of the privileges is that we become co-heirs in the Kingdom of God. Romans 8:17 informs us, "Now if we are children, then we are heirs—heirs of God and co-heirs with Christ."

There is the privilege of suffering for our faith. Probably one of the privileges we wish we could ignore, and many do, is the privilege of suffering for Christ. Romans 8:17 adds this phrase, "If indeed we share in his sufferings." Those who have the idea or supposition that one can walk down the aisle in a church, say a few words to a counselor or a pastor, be baptized, and go on living as if nothing ever happened are fooling themselves, but they are not fooling God.

There was an old saying around many years ago, that is very true today: "If you want to dance, you have to pay the fiddler." By the same token, those who are looking for some pie in the sky salvation where they can come to the throne of grace without having practiced their faith, if they have any, and say, "Here I am God, aren't you lucky," are going to hear those terrible words spoken in Matthew 25:41, "Depart from me, you who are cursed, into eternal fire prepared for the devil and his angels." I have heard it said, "What you do is what you believe." If you aren't doing anything, there is a good chance, you aren't believing anything.

There is another privilege presented to us by Paul in Romans 8:17c, "In order that we may share in His glory."

What a day that will be when we stand before him and hear those words, "Well done thou good and faithful servant." The Bible says when he comes to get us our rewards will be in his hands.

Revelation 22:12: "Behold, I am coming quickly and my reward is with me, to render to every man according to what he has done." Contrary to some discussions I've heard that were strictly carnal and materialistic, there is a description I'm clinging to. In 1 Corinthians 2:9 NIV, "No eye has seen, nor ear heard, no mind has conceived what God has prepared for those who love him."

There is the privilege of eternal life. Romans 6:23, "The wages of sin is death, but the gift of God is eternal life in Jesus Christ our Lord."

How would you describe eternal life? Someone asked me recently where God came from. I tried to explain his eternal existence this way: It's kind of like a circle. It has no beginning or end. It's hard for most to grasp the idea that something has no beginning.

The simple explanation that God always is takes faith to accept. There is no rational explanation: it's a matter of faith; faith often contradicts rationality. Elton Trueblood, a psychiatrist, theologian, and writer, once said, "Faith is not taking a blind leap into the darkness, but walking carefully in the light we have."(207)

It seems to me, it takes very little faith to walk in the light. For me a better definition of faith is "walking to the edge of light and taking one more step." That is the picture painted in the eleventh chapter of Hebrews.

Romans 8:19 also gives us a great picture of faith, "I consider that our present sufferings are not worth comparing with the glory that will be revealed in us. The creation waits with eager expectation for the sons of God to be revealed."

Christians are overcomers. 1 John 4:4b, "And have overcome them." The apostle Paul reinforces this point in Romans 8:37, "In all these things we are more than conquerors through him who loved us." They are overcomers because they are indwelt by the Holy Spirit of God. 1 John 4:4c, "Because the one who is in you is greater than the one who is in the world."

Christians Have a Special and Unique Communication

1 John 4:6 confirms that when John writes, "We are from God, and whoever knows God listens to us."

Christians receive communication with the King of Kings: Jesus informs us that, "Everyone who listens to the Father and learns from him comes to me" (John 6:45). Therein lies the way of salvation and clarifies the meaning of being called by God to salvation. Jesus makes this very clear in the previous verse when he says: "No one can come to me unless the Father who sent me draws him" (John 6:44). Although this drawing of the Holy Spirit occurs in different ways, it is still the moving power of God within our own soul inviting us to him.

Christians Can Call Upon God for Guidance and in Time of Need

Not only is there communication with God concerning salvation, but for Christian living also. It is my sense, as I work on this manuscript that God is at work inspiring me through the Holy Spirit, to speak words that will lift up, lead, and encourage others while he is glorified through the work. I was once asked, during an interview for pastor of a church, what source I used for my sermons. I answered, "Through inspiration of the Holy Spirit." Some on that committee seemed to see that as the wrong answer. It is my understanding and persuasion that if the message is not God inspired, it cannot be a message from God. During an extension class from the Southern Baptist Convention several years ago, I was privileged to have a text book by Ilion T. Jones. Many of the statements in that book claim leadership of the Holy Spirit. I am thoroughly convinced of its validity and unconditionally surrendered to it. That doesn't mean I always follow instructions, I often go off on my own path, but when I do, there is usually a penalty for it. I remember most vividly Jones's definition of a sermon. He described a sermon as, "God's message to his people strained through a human personality." (208) I still believe that.

Because there is a common spiritual bond between Christians, there is also an avenue of communication. Christians have the common bond of having been born again through the grace of God and therefore belong to the same family, have the same Father, and are looking forward to the same future.

Teaching is issued and received through the channel of love. There is a mutual love of God and a mutual love for others and because of that there is a spiritual drive within each teacher to speak the truth of God for the benefit of those who will hear.

There is a drawing desire on the part of the one being taught. There is that hunger for righteousness spoken of in Matthew 5:6. There is a desire for a closer walk with Jesus who is our Savior and Lord.

Children of the world worship and follow worldly ways and worldly things. John describes them this way: "They are of the world" (1 John 4:5). This explanation is given from Barnes Notes: "This was one of the marks by which those who had the spirit of the antichrist might be known. They belonged not to the church of God, but to the world; they lived for it." (209)

We are admonished in 1 John 2:15, "Do not love the world or anything in the world."

I visited a Sunday morning Bible study class recently where money was the exclusive topic of the day and celebrating, among other things, fishing and performing labor as rewards in heaven for our being a "Christian" in this lifetime.

Another pastor attempted to point out that tithing involves more than money, but he was informed that all they were talking about on that day was money. This speaks to the latter half of 1 John 4:6, "He who is not from God does not listen to us."

Jesus dealt with those who were interested in money more than the "more important" things pertaining to righteousness: "Woe to you teachers of the law and Pharisees, you hypocrites! You give a tenth of your spices—mint, dill, and cumin. But you have neglected the more important matters of the law—justice, mercy and faithfulness. You should have practiced the latter, without neglecting the former." (210)

When that Bible study teacher, spoken of previously, and those who agreed with him began talking about recreational fishing and continuing in their vocation when they get to heaven, if they do, I was reminded of the scripture found in Ecclesiastes 12:13. After he had tried everything imaginable and some beyond, he made this statement: "Now all has been heard; here is the conclusion of the matter. Fear God and keep his commandments for this is the whole duty of man." One of the great verses that bring me encouragement is found in 1 Corinthians 2:9 KJV, "But as it is written, eye hath not seen, nor ear heard, neither have entered into the heart of man, the things God hath prepared for them that love him."

John says one of the most important things we can do is listen to instruction.

Have you ever known someone who was sure they had all the answers? The Gnostics of whom John was writing evidently had that problem. They worshipped knowledge as if it were a god. It seemed academic achievement was the epitome of spirituality as far as they were concerned. Paul made it clear in Philippians that the purpose of knowledge is service to others.

An elite or condescending attitude has no place in Christianity. Jesus set the pattern; Paul described his attitude like this: "Who being in very nature God, did not consider equality with God something to be grasped, but made himself nothing, taking the very nature of a servant" (Philippians 2:7).

CHAPTER 20

Light on the Path of Righteous Is Revealed by a Powerful Love

1 John 4:7–11

J ohn spoke of love in three different representations of how love fits into the Christian life. In chapter 2:7–11, he discusses love as proof of authentic fellowship. In 3:10–17, it is represented as an authentic relationship. Here, he presents the correlation of love for others and love for God as each relates to the personal relationship of the believer with God as a channel of the unselfish, all-powerful love of God for mankind.

In a quote found in The Treasury of Religious Quotations published by the *Reader's Digest*, Gail McGrew made this contribution: "True love—the kind we ordinarily attribute to God—is foolish, risky, and absolutely necessary. It brings to a standstill the ordinary games of distrust." (211)

In the fourth chapter of 1 John, he deals with that which goes beyond the idea of being risky or foolish into a love that is powerful because its source is the all-powerful God. Jakob Boehme expresses this opinion of love by saying: "Love, being the highest principle, is the virtue of all virtues, from whence they flow forth. Love, being the greatest majesty, is the power of all powers, from whence they severally operate." (212)

The power of love is found in its selflessness. John points out that the powerful love is a shared love: "Dear friends, let us love one another" (1 John 4:7)

A professional basketball player reportedly bragged recently on television that he had "made love to ninety-nine women." A young law student testified before certain people her desire to be supplied with "free" birth control pills so she can save the money to go to law school. Allow me to say to her the best remedy for birth control is to abstain from social sex.

These and others often use the word love in a nonchalant and dismissive way. They are obviously not involved in acts of love but the more animalistic exercise known universally as sex. On the other hand, there are many individuals who are searching for and practicing authentic and sincere love. John is calling for that kind of love.

Paul outlines a realistic and vivid picture of love in 1 Corinthians: "Love is patient and is kind. It does not envy, it does not boast, it is not proud. It is not rude, it is not self- seeking, it is not easily angered; it keeps no record of wrongs. Love does not delight in evil but rejoices with the truth. It always protects, it always trusts, always hopes, always perseveres." (213)

Then he adds this great promise in the first part of verse eight: "Love never fails." All the features of this great picture have a social aspect because each one, although unspoken, has others in mind.

One of the greatest features of agape love is it's putting others first because the basic motive is that of giving. Unlike eros love, which considers self above all else, agape love (Christian love) is made more powerful by giving it away. John 3:16 demonstrates the love of God by stating his giving the ultimate gift: "For God so loved the world that he gave his only begotten Son . . ." This agape love cements Christians together and binds them into a fellowship that can be described as a bond of love because it is made up of love for God and love for others.

J. Vernon McGee outlines three different kinds of "love" in his book on 1 John and emphasizes the difference in agape love and the other two types.

"Again, may I say that the word for love here is not eros; John is not talking about sex. All through this section, the word for love is agape love. It is not sentimental, it is not sexual, and it is not social love. It is supernatural love." (214)

There are a few Greek words that need some explaining here for the benefit of the reader. The Greek word *eros* refers to self-love and is used often to refer to sexual or promiscuous love. The Greek word *philia* refers to family or social love and the word *agape* refers to the supernatural selfless love that is a part of the life of every one who has been born again and lives the life of an authentic Christian. John MacArthur supports the position of McGee and says, "Unlike emotional, physical, or friendship love, agape love is the love of self-sacrificing service." (215)

We are informed in 1 John 4:7c, "Everyone who loves has been born of God and knows God."

I remember a sermon preached by Dr. W. A. Criswell, many years ago, as nearly as I can remember it was pertaining to the Latin phrase, "Ta Stigma Ta," using Galatians 6:17, "I bear in my body the marks of the Lord Jesus." (216)

In the marginal comments, the NKJB concerning this verse elaborates the suffering Paul endured for the gospel.

A Powerful Love Has a Powerful Testimony

The testimony of every authentic Christian is the powerful love we have been discussing up to this point. Jesus says: "By this all men will know you are my disciples" (John 13:35). John says "Everyone who loves has been born of God and knows God." (1 John 4:7c).

Paul's physical body carried the hard evidence of his allegiance to the Lord Jesus, the marks of harsh persecution: "Are they servants of Christ? (I must be out of my mind to talk like this.) I am more. I have worked much harder, been in prison more frequently, been flogged more severely, and been exposed to death again and again. Five times I received from the Jews forty lashes minus one. Three times I was beaten with rods, once I was stoned, three times I was shipwrecked, I spent a day and a night in the open sea, I have been constantly on the move, I have been in danger from rivers, in danger from bandits, in danger from my own countrymen, in danger from the Gentiles; in danger in the city, in danger in the country, in danger at sea and in danger from false brothers." (217)

Some of us possess some of the same marks, or different ones for the same reason, but there is another more positive and more lasting mark of authenticity for the real Christian. The "birth mark of authentic Christians is one we have discussed before, but more information is added here as we perceive the birthmark to be evidence of powerful love. Harold T. Bryson calls it a "birthmark" as do some others and he confirms this perspective and states: "John proceeded to describe a noticeable distinctive of God's children. The believers' spiritual birthmark is a powerful love for one another." (218)

The *World Book Encyclopedia* describes a birthmark as: "A blemish on the skin which is usually present at birth." (219)

Guy H. King points out, "It is a sign of a newly born body that it breathes life; likewise, it is the mark of a newborn soul that it breathes love." (220)

A Powerful Love Has God for Its Source

This is a love that has an indescribable force behind it. It's the kind of love that drives a mother or father into a burning building to save their child. It is the kind of love that will cause a soldier to give his life on a field of combat. It is the kind of love God has given for and to every born again Christian. There is no explanation for it; it just is. It is like the wind Jesus spoke of: "The wind blows where it wishes and you hear the sound of it, but do not know where it comes from and where it is going; so is everyone who is born of the Spirit."

1 John 4:8 informs us that, "God is love." This verse shows us that God is not just a container of love or an issuer of love, he is love, and therefore the source for the kind of agape love spoken of earlier. Love is revealed by action. One way we know about God's love is the giving of his only begotten Son for our sins. 1 John 4:10 clearly

states, "This is love: not that we loved God but that he loved us and sent his Son as an atoning sacrifice for our sins." The phrase "atoning sacrifice" in the NIV is translated in the KJV and some other versions another way. Instead of the words atoning sacrifice there is one word—*propitiation.*

Propitiation is a word I have struggled with for a long time. It is not only hard to say the meaning escapes many of us. It really describes the mercy of God for us. J. Vernon McGee informs us that it means "mercy seat." He says, "It is the same as the Old Testament word *atonement,* meaning 'to cover.' (221) It is the implication behind the construction in the Temple of the Holy of Holies. The lid on top of the Ark of the Covenant was decorated with many ornaments and crowned with two cherubim facing each other and looking down upon the lid. That lid was called the mercy seat. It was in the Holy of Holies. At the mercy seat Israel came to face God seeking mercy. Once a year, the high priest came to sprinkle blood on the mercy seat and plead for the forgiveness of the sins for the people of Israel. Hebrews 10:1–7 points out the ineffectiveness of those Old Testament offerings."

"The law is only a shadow of the good things that are coming—not the realities themselves. For this reason, it can never, by the same sacrifices repeated endlessly year after year, make perfect those who draw near to worship. If it could, would they have stopped being offered? For the worshipers, would have been cleansed once for all and would no longer have felt guilty for their sins. But those sacrifices are an annual reminder of sins, because it is impossible for the blood of bulls and goats to take away sins, therefore when Christ came into the world, he said: Sacrifice and offering you did not desire but a body you prepared for me; with burnt offerings and sin offerings you were not pleased. Then I said, here I am—it is written about me in the scroll—I have come to do your will O God. And by that will, we have been made holy through the sacrifice of the body of Jesus Christ once for all." (222)

That sprinkling of blood occurred on the cross of Calvary. The blood of Jesus Christ was shed on the cross as an everlasting offering for the forgiveness of the sin of everyone who accepts him as

Lord and Savior. That act of mercy was initiated by the all-powerful, all-loving God of the universe.

A Powerful Love Begins with God

God is not only the source. He is also the force.

I have often heard individuals say, "He makes me so mad," or words to that effect. I was taught in my psychology classes that no one can make you mad or angry; that's a decision you make on your own. Experience has proven that correct to a certain extent; but it is also taught by psychologists, there are certain reflexes and emotions present at birth. It is my contention, and experience, that the innate forces that are spoken of are put there by God for survival. If that is true, love also has God for its source. Evidence of that can be found throughout creation, both in man and other creatures. 1 John 4:10, "This is love. Not that we loved God but that he loved us and sent his Son as an atoning sacrifice for our sins."

Consider the waterwheel and the power of moving water, then consider the comparison between moving, flowing water and the realization that Christians are channels through whom flows the love of God. The *World Book Encyclopedia* informs us, "The use of water power is hundreds of years old. The first devices were comparatively simple. A platform was built by the side of a stream and attached a wheel which the water pushed against. When the water struck the blade of the wheel, it turned, and power from the wheel could be used to run simple machinery. At first this power was used for lifting water from a river for grinding wheat between heavy stones, which were turned by the wheel. Even after man learned how to use other sources of power, such as windmills and the power in coal to run steam engines, he continued to use the power of water wherever possible. When we speak of the potential power of a river, we usually mean the power that the ordinary minimum flow of the stream (95 percent of the time) exerts on a machine that is 100 percent efficient. The potential water power of the entire world has been estimated at 657,000,000 horsepower." (223)

Wow! That's a lot of power! There seems to be legitimate grounds to compare God's love, as it flows through Christians who are channels for it, with the power found in flowing water because love, like water, can empower and move others to do great things. If the love of God empowered Christians to propagate the gospel the way flowing water is used to furnish power for great engines and furnish much of the energy for America, a great revival would take place.

God is the perfect example of love John not only declares that love begins with God, he declares that God is the perfect example of love: "Dear friends, if this is the way God loved us, we ought to love one another" (1 John 4:11).

Jesus said in John 15:12, "Love each other as I have loved you." That commandment becomes possible when we recognize that God is the inertia (moving force) that causes his powerful love to flow through the spiritual veins of every authentic Christian who claims Jesus Christ as Lord and Savior. 1 John 4:12 informs us that, "No one has ever seen God; but if we love one another, God lives in us and his love is made complete in us."

That's the kind of love seen in the behavior of people like retired pastor Richard Stevens, who travels to countries like China and India, risking his life for the glory and the love of an almighty God. That's the kind of love you can see in people like Rhonda and Marty who took a group from Oklahoma to Colorado, and even Italy, on a mission trip to another church and of thousands of parents and other adults and young people who give of their time and money to spread the gospel to others next door and around the world. Love is indeed made more powerful as it flows from Christians to others.

CHAPTER 21

Light on the Path of Righteousness Reveals Ways of Knowing

1 John 4:12 to 5:2

We can know because he has given us his Spirit. Harold T. Bryson informs his readers, "John wrote to give assurance to bewildered believers." He goes on to say, "Perhaps there is no greater section in the Bible on Christian certainty than 1 John and especially 1 John 4:13 to 5:5." (224)

Although our text covers 1 John 4:12 to 5:2, it certainly could cover those verses in one way or another. Experience and observation have confirmed the remarks of Dr. Bryson when he says: "Questions arise periodically within believers which cause doubts. Rationalism produces doubt. Skepticism encourages doubt. Agnosticism causes one to not be sure. Moral permissiveness raises many questions. Science and technology want observable answers. One of our greatest needs is to make sure periodically of our Christian standing." (225)

Even in the face of all those obstacles, John gives us the good news: "We can know."

One of the ways we can know we have the gift of salvation and eternal life is pointed out in 1 John 4:13 when John states, "We know that we live in him and he in us, because he has given us of his Spirit." This term confuses many because they look for a significant, earth-shaking revelation or event or emotional moment indicating rebirth and some can point to that kind of experience. But here I would like to point out once again, "It's not how high one jumps when he or she is saved but how one lives that proves authenticity.

J. Vernon McGee addresses the subject of conversion this way: "Once you have been born again, how do you know you have been born again? Do you have some great overwhelming experience? Do you enter an ecstatic state? Not necessarily; some people do, I'm told, but that is not the usual procedure. 'Whosoever believeth that Jesus is the Christ is born of God: and everyone that loveth him that begat loveth him also that is begotten of him.' When you trust the Lord Jesus Christ, you are born again." (226)

Acknowledgement is evidence of his indwelling Spirit. There is an acknowledgement of the need for faith.

It is interesting that John begins by pointing out our knowing that we know with an acknowledgement: 1 John 4:12 points out that, "No one has ever seen God." Although both here and at the beginning of this writing he confirms that he has physically touched, felt and experienced Christ during his days on earth, 1 John 1:1–3; 4:14, "And we have seen and testify that the Father has sent his Son to be the Savior of the world." We are still consigned to accepting, believing and propagating love as the evidence of God's existence and our participation in making that love complete. John makes that very clear when he declares, "God lives in us and his love is made complete in us" (1 John 4:12b).

Although acknowledgement that we have not seen Jesus in the flesh therefore visual confirmation of his existence and relevance to our life cannot be possible; with that acknowledgement through faith comes the positive acknowledgement of spiritual experiencing that is a reality of Christian life. 1John 4:15 points out the necessity of acknowledgement that Jesus is the son of God and says, "If anyone acknowledges that Jesus is the Son of God, God lives in him and he in God."

One definition for learning is that it is knowledge that becomes a part of you and changes your behavior. We have been exposed to information without measure in our lifetime. Some say, everything we have seen and heard remains with us to one extent or another, but only that which we have retained and allowed to affect our existence is relevant, or for that matter, really remembered.

Learning about Jesus and his salvation is more than words. It is inner admission that Jesus is the Son of God who walked among us, died on the cross in our place, was raised from the dead and is coming again. That is reason enough for heartfelt celebration. No wonder Paul could say, "The fruit of the Spirit is Love, joy, peace." What a day that will be when our Jesus we shall see! But greater news is available, we can rejoice now as we realize the certainty of his presence and his promises. There are those who say, "I know Jesus," but walk in the ways of the world. John makes it very clear throughout this letter, if you really know Jesus, his Spirit abides in you and your heart's desire is to please him with your lifestyle because "he has given us of his Spirit."

Acknowledgement is confession of spiritual communication with God. The apostle Paul gives us the formula for salvation in Romans 10:9 when he states, "If we confess with our mouth that Jesus is Lord and believe in our heart that God raised him from the dead, we shall be saved."

I must confess, I am a person of spontaneity. That isn't always good, but it is an illustration of an individual who has believed in his heart that Jesus is Lord and is compelled by that realization to tell others. That, sometimes, is neither popular nor comfortable, but it is always a force within one who has experienced authentic conversion and really believes Jesus is Lord. I must admit I could be a little more discreet, but confession, not a one-time going down front and mumbling something to the pastor or counselor kind of confession, but continual confession, both verbally and with lifestyle, is a part of being a real Christian. When Paul said, "If we confess with our mouth," I believe he meant anytime, anywhere as well as the profession of faith initially made when we declare and confess our salvation for the first time.

We know we are saved when we rely on God's love. In 1 John 4:16, John offers assurance with these words: "And so we know and rely on the love God has for us."

His is a love to be relied upon as we travel through this life as his ambassadors.

Guy H. King writes of the Christian as having three positions: "We are in this world as aliens." (227)

John confirms that position when he, describes our position as ambassadors this way: "In this world we are like him" (1 John 4:17). An ambassador is one who represents his government and country in a foreign land. In John 15:9, Jesus informed his disciples: "If you belonged to the world, it would love you as its own. As it is, you do not belong to the world."

On the other hand, Paul tells us we are Ambassadors and outlines the purpose and function of an ambassador: "So from now on we regard no one from a worldly point of view. Though we once regarded Christ in this way, we do so no longer. Therefore, if anyone is in Christ, he is a new creation; the old has gone, the new has come! All this is from God, who reconciled us to himself through Christ and gave us the ministry of reconciliation. That God was reconciling the world to himself in Christ not counting men's sins against them and has us to us the message of reconciliation."

Then he says in verse 20, "We are therefore Christ's ambassadors, as though God were making an appeal through us." (228)

Guy H. King describes an ambassador like this: "Earthly monarchs have their ambassadors in other lands to represent them at the foreign court—standing for dignities and rights of their sovereign, keeping their government in touch with anything affecting the interests of their country, speaking in the name of their ruler, and with all his power behind them." (229)

If that is an accurate description of an ambassador, and if we are in fact "ambassadors for Christ" as Paul says we are, that makes the Christian very powerful and very responsible.

We know we are saved when we live in "the love house."

Guy H. King talks about the Christian in the position of "living in the love house" and points out the scripture in 1 John 4:16. Although he doesn't use that whole verse, it seems to fit perfectly with the picture of "dwelling in the love house." (231)

In its entirety, 1 John 4:16 states, "And so we know and rely on the love God has for us. God is love. Whoever lives in love lives in God, and God in him."

There is that phrase again: "We know." When we know the love of God to the certainty that we trust and rely on him, that is another source of assurance that we have salvation in him. That knowing brings us into a new perspective—a new sense of existence. Because we rely on the love of God, and because we live in the dwelling place called "the love house," there is a sense of fulfillment and completeness available to us. With that sense of who we are comes a lack of fear. The fear of living is cancelled along with the fear of judgment. The commentaries I have read discuss the fear of judgment and that certainly needs to be dealt with and is dealt with here in these verses. First John 4:18a informs us that, "There is no fear in love. But perfect love drives out fear," and verse 18b makes it clear that the day of judgment is a reality, and the world is not our permanent home; therefore, love of God dictates our full service to him and dedication to his kingdom.

"Do you not know that your body is the temple of the Holy Spirit, who is in you, whom you have received from God? You are not your own; you have been bought at a price. Therefore, honor God with your body." (231)

Light on the path of righteousness reveals a reason for love. God is not only love itself, the force of love, and the example for Christian love; he is also the reason for love. John informs us: "We love because he first loved us" (1John 4:19).

2 Peter 1:3–4 explains what is involved in the statement, "He first loved us," very clearly. He gives us sort of a list of the gifts that come with God's having loved us. First, he tells us in 2 Peter 1:3 that his divine power has given us everything we need for life and godliness through our knowledge of him who called us by his own glory and goodness.

In 1 John 4:19, John makes the very cogent point that before we can live a lifestyle of love, we must experience God's love. He makes that point very clear in verse nineteen by saying, "We love because he first loved us. Without our experiencing the love of God in our own lives there would be no source for the agape love Christians are called upon to give." There is a saying, "You can't get water from an empty well." That statement has been applied to the need of preachers to be involved in constant research, prayer and Bible study. It also applies to Christian love. It is impossible for one to express authentic love if love is not present within. Someone once said, "A good preacher should be prayed up read up, and ready to stand up anytime, any-place." I believe that to be true; it does not, however, just apply to preachers, nor to preaching. It applies to every Christian. Every Christian should be willing to conduct a loving ministry any time in any situation. That begins with a dedication that can only come from an individual who has experienced God's love and is ready to pass it on to others.

2 Peter clarifies John's statement by giving us more than the above listed gifts. He also gave us great and precious promises that allows us to partake of and participate in his divine nature. 2 Peter 1:4 informs us, "Through these he has given us his very great and precious promises so that through them you may participate in the divine nature and escape the corruption in the world caused by evil desires."

Wow! Don't you see? That is why we love! We love because we have a divine nature. 1 John 4:13 says, "We know that we live in him and he in us because he has given us of his Spirit." That's a divine nature! That's the nature of love. God has not only given us every-thing we need for life and godliness; he has empowered within us a divine desire to love.

Because he loves us, we extend our love to others. That list of gifts bestowed upon those who are undeserving of his great love cou-pled with the divine nature bestowed upon all authentic Christians is an example and a motivator, not only to return his love but to share it with others regardless of their attitude or behavior toward us.

Barnes Notes informs us, "If we just love him for what he has done for us or because he has shown some act of love toward us we are being selfish." (232)

Jesus himself spoke against that in Matthew 5:46–47: "For if you love those who love you what reward will you get? Are not even the tax collectors doing that? And if you greet only your brothers, what are you doing more than others? Do not even the pagans do that?"

Barnes informs us, "If you love those that love you, you are selfish, you are not disinterested; it is not genuine love for the character, but love for the benefit; and you deserve no commendation. The very publicans would do the same." (233)

Barnes further states, "It cannot be believed that John meant to teach that that is the only reason of our love for God." That is made clear in Matthew 5:43–44 when Jesus said: "You have heard it said, 'Love your neighbor and hate your enemy.' But I tell you, love your enemies and pray for those who persecute you." His point is actually clarified in the following verses when they are viewed in context. When John said, "Our love is caused by God's love," he meant more than that he had given us everything we need in an earthly or physical sense. (234)

Keith Miller, pastor of First Baptist Church, Enid, Oklahoma, described the conduct of love during a message he delivered recently. Although he used a different text as a basis for his message, he presented four points that are pertinent in 1 John 4:19–21. I am going to use the main points of that sermon and elaborate on them.

1. Christians Extend God's love through forgiveness. Colossians 3:13, "Bear with each other and forgive whatever grievances you may have against one another. Forgive as the Lord forgave you."

   When we begin to discuss forgiveness of others, we must first be sure we have forgiven ourselves. 1 John 1:9 states, "If we confess our sins, he is faithful and just to forgive us our sins and cleanse us from all unrighteousness." I wonder how many of us are struggling with the task of forgiveness of others when we have not forgiven ourselves. One of my professors from years ago, used a phrase I have modified to fit my own beliefs established through years of experience and observation: "The past is a thief that robs today of its joy and tomorrow of its promise." I must confess I'm one of those who is guilty of returning to the past from time to time when I submit to the power and influence of Satan. But he can't keep me there. My sins have been forgiven. Today is a new day. I'm a new creation in Christ Jesus.

Forgiveness of others is made easier when we realize we also make mistakes or jump to erroneous conclusions or come up with mistaken judgment from time to time. The apostle Paul tells us we should be careful about correcting others because we could be next.

2. Christians become involved in other people's problems. We are instructed in Galatians 6:2, "Carry each other's burdens and in this way, you will fulfill the law of Christ."

    "Can I help?" ought to be one of the phrases most used in a Christian's vocabulary. When we encounter someone who is cross or seems angry, it would be in the best interest of Christian love to spend a little bit of time listening. That person could be in the middle of some tragic situation. Sometimes mental or physical pain can be mistaken for anger. Perhaps he or she just needs someone to listen. I have seen many people, including preachers and pastors, in my time who were great talkers but very poor listeners. I recently had lunch with a young man to discuss a situation in my life. I listened to him for almost two hours and only took a few moments to discuss my own ideas. It is my opinion that he needed to talk. I hope and pray he was helped by my behavior during our conversation.

3. Christians perform loving deeds. It is my personal observation that it's hard to love a porcupine. At first glance that might seem absurd, but most of us know, or have known, someone who has very prickly behavior. When we try to get close to them, they say or do something offensive or hurtful. Sometimes we can all be porcupines in one way or another.

We were told when we were young that porcupines throw their quills to attack their opponent, but in truth, they use their quills as a defense mechanism. That is also true of people. Sometimes they reject efforts to befriend them or help them because they are afraid of being hurt. They reject friendly people because of fear of being rejected. That is why it is important to look beyond their behavior to see their need and help them through Christian love and understanding.

4. Christians expect the best from others. Suspicion rules the day for many of us these days. For some, it has taken over their life. If you offer to help, it is sometimes refused because they are expecting the worst to happen. The media has done much to cultivate distrust and uncertainty by offering unwarranted and sometimes erroneous advice about strangers and adults. Have you stopped to think, "If child abuse by strangers were that common, it wouldn't be news." Most child abuse, especially sexual abuse, occurs by the hand of a relative or member of the family. Does that mean parents should stop trusting each other? We should expect the best of everyone. If they prove us wrong, we should try to help them in the situation. In my ministry, I have known two young men who killed their babies. Both men had the same problem: although their situations were different, they both became frustrated because of ignorance and the lack of support from those who claimed to love them. I stood by each one as he proceeded through trial, sentencing and serving of the prison term allotted. We prayed together and counseled each other and even cried together until it was over. They later raised a family and became "normal" parents. Whatever that is. Even in their situation, there were those who loved them and expected the best from them. Those expectations carried them through the hard times and made them better prepared for

life. I wish I could say they became Christians, but neither of them had done so when I last saw them.

What you do is what you believe; all else is just religious talk. Please allow me to begin commentary on 1 John 4:20 with a disclaimer. Two of my very best friends are North American Indians. One is a Creek who is the pastor of Indian Nations Baptist Church in Seminole, Oklahoma; the other is a Seminole who is retired from the ministry and living on a creek bank in the backwoods east of Collinsville, Oklahoma. As far as I know, I am a full-blooded Englishman. I have spent twenty years of my life in the army. During that time, I have been stationed in many countries throughout the world, including Vietnam, Korea, Germany, and Hawaii. I have yet to see a red person. I have yet to see a black person. I have seen some who have a lighter complexion than I have but say they are black. Black is a color. Red is a color. White is a color.

Color is a term that separates and prevents people of different races from coming together. Although you might view my position as ludicrous, it is my contention that if we could agree that we are different shades of the same color, loving our brother would be much easier for many of us. Perhaps an even better solution is to consider color an irrelevant factor in determining who our brother is. As it is now, however, many who claim to be good Christian men and women have prejudice in their heart toward those of another race.

Let's look at Malachi 2:10 at the question asked every one of us must answer. "Have we not all one Father? Did not one God create us? Why do we profane the covenant of our fathers by breaking faith with one another? 1John 4:20 makes this declaration: "If anyone says, 'I love God,' yet hates his brother, he is a liar for anyone who does not love his brother, whom he has seen, cannot love God whom he has not seen."

God created us all. We all have our faults. In Romans 3:23, the apostle Paul reminds us, "All have sinned and fall short of the glory of God."

It is possible for one to plead ignorance, as the scribe did when Jesus told him to love his neighbor as himself and ask that inane question, "Who is my brother?" Is it not Adam the head of the human race? Do we not all claim him as the beginning of the human race? We must, if we accept God as creator and sustainer of the universe. If that is true, we are to love everyone. We don't have to like their ways, but we can still love them and try to lead them to accept Christ and love others.

If there is a lingering anger or dislike for others, it blocks the path to the kingdom. That kind of anger could be described as the grudge kind of anger. I knew two brothers one time who had been angry with each other for over five years over a piece of land; there is no room for that kind of anger in the heart of one who loves because God has directed us to love one another.

Ephesians 4:26 addresses lingering anger or grudging behavior this way: "In your anger do not sin. Do not let the sun go down while you are still angry."

To love is a command. Previously, we discussed the subject of love was an indicator and a sign of salvation; now John says, "And he has given us this command. Whoever loves God must love his brother" (1 John 4:21).

According to the *Holman Illustrated Bible Dictionary*, Gnosticism, which was the primary purpose for the writing of 1 John, was an heretical structure of beliefs which resulted in the church being, "torn by heated debates over the issues." (235)

That kind of behavior is the exact opposite of godly love.

A simple observation I have heard in the past is, "It takes two to make an argument." It is impossible to present an authentic loving atmosphere in the church when a member is playing a game or claiming to be someone who has all the answers. Arguments can only come with an attitude of self-importance. Paul had an answer for that: "If you have any encouragement from being united with Christ, if any comfort from his love, if any fellowship with the Spirit, if any tenderness and compassion then make my joy complete by being like-minded; having the same love, being one in spirit and purpose. Do nothing out of selfish ambition or vain conceit, but in humility consider others better than yourselves." (236)

Near the end of chapter two of Philippians in verse fourteen he says, "Do everything without complaining or arguing."

Keith Miller made a very valid point in the message mentioned previously when he said, "Love is a choice." John makes it clear to his readers, the ultimate choice is yours to make. It is perfectly legitimate to accept this statement as being based on the statement Jesus made in John 13:34, "A new command I give you: love one another; as I have loved you, so you must love one another." It is a shame for those who profess Christianity to fight and argue amongst themselves and to bear grudges and express dislike for others. It is also a witness for evil.

Love is more than a choice; it is a message to the world. Jesus said in John 13:35, "By this all men will know you are my disciples, if you love one another."

Can others see Jesus in you? Love is the way to express his presence in our life. No matter how religious you might become nor how closely you follow the Ten Commandments, if your life does not reflect the love of Jesus for others, you need to examine the authenticity of your relationship with him. The apostle Paul made that very clear when he makes this declaration: "If I speak with the tongues of men and angels, but have not love, I am only a sounding gong or a clanging symbol. If I have the gift of prophecy and can fathom all mysteries and all knowledge, and I have a faith that can move mountains, but I have not love, I am nothing. If I give all I possess to the poor and surrender my body to the flames, but have not love, I gain nothing." (237)

Loving Jesus because he is the Son of God is proof of salvation. It is impossible to be saved and not love and recognize Jesus as the Son of God. A strong case has been made for the connection of believing that Jesus is the Son of God. 1 John 5:1 makes it abundantly clear that you can't have one without the other. He says, "Everyone who believes that Jesus is the Christ (the anointed one) is born of God, and everyone who loves the Father, loves his child as well."

Barnes notes points out that, "It cannot be supposed that a mere intellectual acknowledgment of the proposition that Jesus is the Messiah is all that is meant, for that is not a proper meaning of the word believe in the Scriptures." If one recognizes Jesus as indeed the Son of God in the scriptural sense of that word, then we must see him as an equal part of the trinity and deserving of our love in same sense as does God. (133)

Guy H. King discusses two different views concerning this verse about the equal love for God and his Son Jesus Christ and says, "We have heard the old saying, 'Love me, love my dog.'" (239)

The idea here is similar: Love God, love his child.

Saint Augustine held that this phrase referred to Christ, "The only begotten of the Father," John 1:14; but the late Bishop Westcott felt that the whole context was against that interpretation, and that it must mean, not the Son but the sons." I'm not qualified to enter this discussion with any degree of credibility, but all the translations and reference materials I have studied point to Jesus the child.

The point of John's letter comes home once again. It is written to the Gnostics and those who wish to deny Jesus as the Christ of God. John's purpose is to refute their claim and firmly establish the deity of Jesus and his relationship with the Father. The *Holman Illustrated Bible Dictionary* informs us that: "Irenaeus reported that one of the reasons John wrote his Gospel was to refute the views of Cerinthus, an early gnostic. Over against the gnostic assertion that the true God would not enter our world, John stressed in his Gospel that Jesus was God's incarnate Son." (240

John saw the love of Jesus so important that he repeatedly expressed it as proof of salvation. In this passage of Scripture, he informs us that obedient love is proof of salvation. When we live in obedience, we are expressing our love for him. John confirms that point with this statement in 1 John 5:2, "This is how we know that we love the children of God by loving God and carrying out his commands."

I love you can be so many empty words; even in churches. Talking about being a loving congregation and loving those of the congregation can be two different things completely. Paul's first letter to the Corinthians suggests a church who was struggling with many differences, and, in some cases, outright sinful attitudes and behavior.

In chapter twelve of First Corinthians, Paul describes the church as the body of Christ. One of my daughters has rheumatoid arthritis. A doctor explained it to her this way: "It is the body at war with itself." Some churches resemble that description. One of John's criticisms concerning some of the churches in Revelation was that they "had lost their first love." Guy H. King says, "The apostle seems to be quite unable to get away from the subject of love—he conceives it to be of such vast and vital importance that all other excellences rest on it or spring from it or are irradiated by it." (241)

There is a distinct possibility that one of the reasons John concentrated so heavily on the theme of love was caused by the fighting and confusion in the church by the Gnostics and the Judaizers.

Some of the confusion in churches today is brought about by those who depart from Scripture and attempt to "modernize" the church. In these days, as then, there must be a strong effort to serve God and love him and others according to his Holy Word.

Obedience to God then, is the test of love in the church. John states, "This is how we know that we love the children of God: by loving God and carrying out his commands." Going your own way or doing your own thing is neither an act of love for the rest of the congregation, nor evidence of love for God.

Harold T. Bryson says, "Union with the Lord leads to an obedience. An experience with the Lord is not just a feeling of rapture or a formal acknowledgment. It is an involvement in obeying his commands. Love and obedience are inseparable. If your love for God and his children are expressed in obedience to the word of God, unity with him and with his children are the inevitable result." (242)

CHAPTER 22

Light on the Path of Righteousness Reveals Overcomers

1 John 5:3–5

Surrender is the first requirement for an overcomer. It is a result of the recognition of Jesus as Lord in 1 John 5:1, "Everyone that believes that Jesus is the Christ is born of God."

Surrender is the beginning of obedience—1 John 5:3a, "For this is the love of God, that we keep his commandments."

Joshua didn't win the battle of Jericho on the seventh day or the seventh time they walked around the city; Joshua won the battle of Jericho the evening he met the commander of the Lord's army: "Now when Joshua was near Jericho, he looked up and saw a man standing in front of him with a drawn sword in his hand. Joshua went up to him and asked, 'Are you for us or against us?' 'Neither,' he replied, 'but as a commander of the army of the Lord I have now come.' Then Joshua fell face down to the ground in reverence, and asked him, 'What message does my Lord have for his servant?'" (243)

Authentic surrender must come with an attitude of humility. Unless there is surrender, true obedience cannot occur. One of the reasons some churches have pseudo Christians is because they lack the humility required for obedience, and the lack of obedience is a clear mark of inauthenticity.

These individuals claim Christianity while they have a proud and rebellious spirit and a prideful lifestyle. For one to be a true overcomer he or she must first perform the act of surrendering his or her life to Christ with true humility. Jesus informs his potential followers in of that requirement in Matthew 16:24, "Then Jesus said to his disciples, 'If anyone would come after me; he must deny himself and take up his cross and follow me.'"

When true surrender happens, the burden of living the Christian lifestyle becomes a joy. John puts it like this: "For this is the love of God, that we keep his commandments: and his commandments are not grievous" (1 John 5:3 ASV).

John MacArthur offers this reason the burdens of Christianity are not "grievous." "Those who love God will obey his law because they want to honor his holy nature. They do so, not out of dread, but out of loving adoration." (244)

There are at least three reasons for joy in the Lord's service: (1) Christians can find joy in service because of the hope of his coming; (2) Christians can find joy in love of God; and (3) Christians can find joy in the love of others. Let us consider each of these reasons for joy in Christian living individually.

There is joy in service because of the hope of his coming.

The New Bible Commentary, based on the commentary by Jamieson, Fausset, and Brown, offers a basis for this joy as: "The stronger our faith, the easier it is to overcome our natural rebellion against God's commands. The believer who finds God's way hard has never grasped by faith his privileges as God's child." (245)

Ephesians 1:13–14 welcomes those who are authentic Christians by informing us, "And you were also included in Christ when you heard the word of truth, the gospel of your salvation. Having believed, you were marked in him with a seal, the promised Holy Spirit, who is a deposit guaranteeing our inheritance until the redemption of those who are God's possession—to the praise of his glory." (246)

There is joy in service because of the love of God.

Adam Clark's commentary on the New Testament says, "No man is burdened with the duties his own love imposes. An old proverb explains the meaning of the apostle's words: 'Love feels no loads.'" (247)

The apostle Paul gives us a reason to hope in his letter to the Romans when he states: "And hope does not disappoint us because God has poured out his love into our hearts by the Holy Spirit, whom he has given us" (Romans 5:5).

There is joy in service because of love for others. This caution is noted in Galatians 5:13, "You, my brothers, were called to be free. But do not use your freedom to indulge the sinful nature, rather serve one another in love."

Surrender is revealed by submission. Many have claimed to have surrendered while planning a way to overcome or subvert the position or directions of their opponent or benefactor, but God sees into the very depth of our existence and knows whether it is authenticity or duplicity.

One of the most memorable scenes, for me, concerning World War Two was seeing the Japanese ruler surrender his sword to the American commanding general on board that ship. The surrender of that sword was an authentic act of surrender because it was an act of submission. When Paul surrendered his life to Jesus on the Damascus Road, his first act was one of submission. Acts 9:8 tells us, "They lead him by the hand to Damascus." When the crowd heard Peter's sermon on the day of Pentecost, they asked the question, "Men and brethren, what shall we do?" (Acts 2:37).

Notice what prompted their question: "They were cut to the heart" by God's word. The only way to become a Christian is through humble submission. The response of Isaiah, after his experience outlined in chapter six of that book was "Here am I send me." To me, that is an act of complete and unconditional submission produced by an authentic surrender.

Submission is evidence of humility. If I asked you if Gideon were an overcomer, you, probably with very little hesitation, would say yes. When we first meet Gideon he is in his father's winepress threshing wheat so the Midianites can't find him. Does that sound like an overcomer?

Doubt prevents submission. Doubt prevented Gideon from realizing that he was an overcomer. We see his doubt in Judges 6:13, "'But, sir,' Gideon replied, 'If the Lord is with us; why has all this happened to us?'" He was sort of asking why the Lord wasn't doing what he was supposed to be doing. Have you ever felt like it was God's fault you were in the predicament you were in? A man in Alabama blamed God for the death of his baby daughter. Consequently, he refused to accept Christ as Savior or even to attend church.

Doubt leads to disobedience. The Israelites had sinned and had been disobedient before the Lord. Look at Judges 6:1 for evidence of that disobedience, "Again the Israelites did evil in the eyes of the Lord, and for seven years he gave them into the hands of the Midianites."

Doubt leads to fear. Gideon was threshing wheat in his father's wine press because he was hiding in fear from the Midianites but God knows where we are at all the time. Judges 6:11 points out that truth by the action of the angel of the Lord, "The angel of the Lord came and sat down under an oak in Oprah that belonged to Joash, the Abiezrite, where his son Gideon was threshing wheat in a winepress to keep it from the Midianites."

Doubt is disbelief. Gideon indicated that he didn't believe the testimony of the Elders when he said: "Where are all the wonders that our fathers told us about?" (Judges 6:13b).

The question is often asked, "How do we know the Bible is true?" The comment is sometimes heard, "The Bible is no longer relevant because times have changed." We must offer that statement with this question: how can the Word of God be irrelevant when the God of the word is still active in our lives? He still answers prayer. He still sustains the world and all that is in it.

God is still relevant and so is his word. Gideon denied the presence of the Lord when he said, "But now the Lord has abandoned us into the hand of Midians" (Judges 6:13c).

Gideon doubted the promise of victory when he voiced doubt of his position and ability: "'But, Lord,' Gideon asked, 'How can I save Israel? My clan is the weakest of Manasseh, and I am least in the family'" (Judges 6:15).

Gideon was suffering from what I have named the "grasshopper complex." The basis of which is taken from the remarks of the Israelites at the entrance to the Promised Land. "We seemed like grasshoppers in their sight" (Numbers 13:33). Their problem and Gideon's problem and the problem many of us have is that our estimate of our own power to overcome is measured by our assessment of our own strength or standing and not realizing by faith that all things are possible with God.

Christians are overcomers because Christ overcame. Jesus informed his disciples of the hardships they would face because of their allegiance to him then he gave them this message of victory: "Be of good cheer, I have overcome the world." (John 16:33).

Those to whom Peter was writing had an anointing from God himself and were looking forward to everlasting life with Jesus, but persecution soon overtook them and they were scattered to surrounding countries and cities. When Peter wrote his first letter, it was addressed to those "scattered throughout Pontus, Galatia, Cappadocia, Asia, and Bythinia." And was designed to assure them that some of the great and precious promises would be for the future: "Praise be to the God and Father of our Lord Jesus Christ! In his great mercy he has given us new birth into a living hope through the resurrection of Jesus Christ from the dead and into an inheritance that can never perish, spoil, or fade—kept in heaven for you." (248)

Looking forward to that promise as real in their lives, these scattered people saw themselves as overcomers. Paul called them, and those of us who receive that same promise: "More than conquerors through him who loved us" (Romans 8:37) "At the time of the encounter of Gideon with the angel of the Lord, he was none of those things."

When John told those to whom he was writing in 1 John 5:4, "For everyone born of God overcomes the world," he was talking to those who were in Christ and had the benefit of his overcoming power. He was talking to those who had been obedient to God, had received the great and precious promises available to believers, spoken of in 2 Peter 1:1–4 Some of those promises are to be granted in heaven in the future.

In Numbers 13:6, two men are featured who were not infected with the grasshopper complex. "Joshua, son of Nun, and Caleb, son of Jephunneh, who were among those who had explored the land, tore their clothes, and said to the entire Israelite assembly, 'The land we passed through and explored is exceedingly good. If the Lord is pleased with us, he will lead us into this land, a land flowing with milk and honey, and will give it to us.'"

By faith, these men knew the war belonged to God and the strength for it lay in his hands. They had seen the manna, they had seen the miracles. They knew as God had provided in the past, he would provide in the future. But apparently, Gideon did not have the benefit of personal experience such as they had enjoyed. In Judges 6:13, Gideon asked the question: "Where are all the wonders that our fathers told us about?"

Doubt must be dealt with. Gideon dealt with his doubt by seeking assurance from a sign. "Gideon replied, 'If now I have found favor in your eyes, give me a sign that it is really you talking to me'" (Judges 6:17).

To compensate for his lack of personal experience, Gideon asked for several signs to establish if the call indeed was coming from God and if it were meant for him. Now, let's ask the question again. Was Gideon an overcomer? He tested the messenger from God. But 1 John 4:1 tells us to test the spirits. Here is something we must look at to make our determination.

Judges 6:12, "When the angel of the Lord appeared to Gideon, he said, 'The Lord is with you, mighty warrior.'" Is it possible that Gideon was an overcomer all the time and just didn't realize it?

He was hiding from the enemy to thresh his wheat; he was not sure if the one who had come to him was really from God or not, and he even voiced doubt of the promises given his forefathers.

On the other hand, notice his reaction when his doubt had been dealt with. He surrendered completely in humility to the will of God.

Faith is the key to victory. John helps us to relate to Gideon's kind of faith when he states, "This is the victory that has overcome the world, even our faith" (1 John 5:4b).

What faith it must have taken to stand against hordes of enemy and break three hundred lanterns and blow trumpets: "Gideon and the hundred men with him reached the edge of the camp at the beginning of the middle watch, just after they had changed the guard. They blew the trumpets and broke the jars that were in their hands. The three companies blew their trumpets and smashed the jars. Grasping the torches in their left hands and holding in their right hands the trumpets they were to blow, they shouted, 'A sword for the Lord and for Gideon!' While each man held his position around the camp, all the Midianites ran crying out as they fled." (250

Gideon had the kind of faith it takes to be an overcomer. Is it possible God knew from the beginning of Gideon's experience that the potential was there? Is it possible that many of us have that same kind of potential but have not realized it because we have not tested it?

I mentioned previously my time spent in a church in Lawton, Oklahoma. That church believed in the power of prayer for healing.

There was a young lady (fifteen years of age at the time) who had leukemia. I left work and took the bus to Oklahoma City Children's Hospital to pray for her. When I finally came into her room and sat on the edge of her bed to pray, I couldn't do it. (251)

Although I was only fifteen at that time, my inability to pray has haunted me for over sixty years. I failed the faith test; yet I see myself as an overcomer because of the many trials, abuses, and tests of faith God has given me the spiritual strength to overcome these last several years

In that situation, my lack of faith prevented my becoming an overcomer. In the case of Gideon, however, his faith made him an overcomer and gave him victory over the opposition. Gideon knew what I did not know at that young and inexperienced age—the war was God's war and it was he who would fight the battle. It was a truth that Joshua was very much aware of.

Have you ever heard of someone winning a war by marching around a city seven days? Joshua had enough faith to do that very thing. The greatest absurdity of all was when Joshua commanded the people, "Shout! For the Lord has given you the city."

If you are one who must have everything figured out before you start, there is a certain amount of absurdity to faith. "Faith is walking to the edge of light and taking one more step."

Saul (Paul) became an overcomer after his surrender on the Damascus road (Acts 9:1–9); Isaiah became an overcomer after his surrender in the temple (Isaiah 6:1–9). Are you an overcomer? Have you yet surrendered your life to Jesus?

Realizing who Jesus is deals with doubt. Recently, during a discussion concerning an Old Testament prophet who had behaved in a way that did not glorify God; an individual said about him, "He was not a man of God. He was a man used of God." I'm not qualified to make that call, neither is he; nor were the Gnostics in Jesus's day who claimed the Holy Spirit came upon him at baptism and departed before the crucifixion. If that were true, of course, Jesus would have been an ordinary man used of God. There is a myriad of scriptures, however, that indicate otherwise. Jesus himself declared, "I tell you the truth." Jesus answered, "Before Abraham was born, I am!" (John 8:58). John referred to Jesus in John 1:29 as "The Lamb of God who takes away the sin of the world."

In 1 John 5:5, John makes a statement of exclusion, but in 1 John 5:1, he makes an inclusive statement: "Everyone who believes that Jesus is the Son of God." That's an inclusive statement addressed to everyone who believes that truth; it includes everyone who authentically believes Jesus is the Son of God.

Now watch! Here John separates those who are not authentic believers in Jesus as the Son of God when he asks the rhetorical question: "Who is it that overcomes the world? Only he who believes that Jesus is the Son of God" (1 John 5:5).

This same verse indicates that those who deny the deity and the everlastingness and the Lordship of Jesus Christ are, not only not overcomers, but neither do they have an inheritance in the kingdom of God. John makes it explicitly clear that only he who believes Jesus is the Son of God can be an overcomer.

Accepting who Jesus is deals with doubt. Romans 10:9 says, "That if you confess with your mouth, 'Jesus as Lord,' and believe in your heart that God raised him from the dead, you will be saved."

Perhaps you have believed in your heart but have not declared (confessed) your faith. There is no such thing as a closet Christian. Confession is required. It is clearly stated in the New King James Version Bible: "For with the heart one believes unto righteousness, and with the mouth confession is made unto salvation" (Romans 10:10).

CHAPTER 23

Light for the Path of Righteousness Is Supplied by Physical Witnesses

1 John 5:6–12

Throughout the history of Christianity, there have been those who were determined to prove either that Jesus was not who he said he was or that he did not exist. Today, some churches are packed with religious people who come as much for social reasons and entertainment as for worship. If some of them were asked how or if they believe that Jesus really existed, they would be hard put to answer from a position of having personally experienced spiritual fellowship with him.

Harold T. Bryson tells us, "Cerinthianism and Docetism are not doctrines that float around today with those names yet similar testimonies circulate about Jesus. Some deny that a man named Jesus ever lived." He mentioned a philosopher, Bertrand Russell who said that he regarded the issue of whether Jesus lived an open question." (252)

A book was published by John Hick in 1977 titled *The Myth of God Incarnate*. The title speaks for itself. There have been many other contemporary deniers who have been very vocal as well. You might be aware of some of them. (253)

As far back as the first century, battles have raged over the identity of Jesus. Harold T. Bryson informs us, "Near the end of the first century in the Roman province of Asia various testimonies were circulated about the person of Jesus. People were making decisions based on these testimonies. On one hand, pagan ideas challenging both the humanity and the divinity of Jesus of Nazareth were circulating. On the other hand, the apostles and others proclaimed the uniqueness of Jesus." (254)

There is an adversarial flavor to the scriptures in 1 John 5:6–12 the adversaries are the Gnostics and others who denied the deity of Christ.

Dr. Bryson paints a word picture of court proceedings (255); if that is the method or procedure used, testimonies are required and witnesses are called. John called three witnesses: the water, the blood of Christ, and the Holy Spirit.

John considered personal knowledge of Jesus's identity of great importance. It is of great importance today. The little hymn that says, "Everybody ought to know who Jesus is" is exactly right.

John says, in effect, if you don't know Jesus, you don't have life. With that in mind, it would be appropriate here to offer some testimony concerning his existence. It is my hope to make the case for who Jesus is by offering some physical and personal testimony concerning his life on earth, then offer some of the divine evidence presented by John.

Evidence of the physical existence of Jesus begins with the testimony of his personal life: his "birthday" is celebrated as "Christmas."

Although it is considered his birth, it is actually his incarnation; that is, his becoming a real human person. The Bible teaches he always was; we have dealt with that in another place.

There were many witnesses to his coming, good and bad. Shepherds, Magi, and even the evil king Herod, contributed to the notoriety of the event.

John said in 1 John 5:6, "This is the one who came." It is important to establish awareness that Jesus had a real life. He "came and dwelt among us" in the flesh. Harold T. Bryson identifies some of the writers who spoke of him and points out with emphasis. "Jesus was real! He is no figment of human imagination."

He came to earth and historians recorded the event. Josephus, the Jewish historian and general, wrote in his, Antiquities of the Jews (AD 93) about the historicity of Jesus. Even Roman writers such as Pliny and Tacitus made reference to the historical Jesus. (256)

He performed many miracles before thousands of people. The miracle of the loaves and the fishes (Mark 6:38–43) is one example. In the fourth chapter of John, many of the citizens of the Samaritan city of Sychar came out to see him and believed in him because of a woman who met him at the well.

The gospels indicate that his crucifixion was well attended. It is marked in history and alluded to even by those who are unbelievers in his great salvation.

"Of course," one might say, "but those are stories from the Bible." Unless one considers the divine testimonies and has been drawn by the Holy Spirit into a personal relationship with Jesus the Christ, all the physical evidence in the world will not convince that individual, therefore, let us consider the evidence John has to offer in 1 John 5:6–12

According to 1 John 5:6, the first witness to be mentioned is water. "This is the one who came by water and by blood—Jesus Christ." Therefore, it seems appropriate to consider it first.

Most of the commentaries I have read indicate that the water mentioned in 1 John 5:6 is referring to the baptism mentioned in Matthew 3:13–17, where all the members of the trinity were present.

"As soon as Jesus was baptized, he went up out of the water. At that moment heaven was opened, and he saw the Spirit of God descending like a dove and lighting on him and a voice saying, 'This is my Son in whom I am well pleased.'" (257)

The water which came from his side at his crucifixion is considered a possibility. Matthew Henry (258) and J. Vernon McGee seem to be, to some extent, among the exceptions to the baptism perspective. They indicate the possibility that the mixture of water and blood which flowed from Jesus' side at the crucifixion could be the reference in 1 John 5:6 (258), *The Beacon Bible Commentary* says,

"The water and the blood have been given many interpretations. The one already mentioned, equating them with baptism and crucifixion, is the most tenable." (259)

Although there doesn't seem to be much support for the position; one thought has been presented, that is that Jesus was referring to the water present at the time of natural birth. If this is the case, it would fit in very well with the theme he was presenting to Nicodemus when he said, "Flesh gives birth to flesh but the Spirit gives birth to the spirit" (John 3:6) and fits very well with his assertion in John 3:5, "I tell you the truth, no one can enter the kingdom of God unless he is born of the water and of the spirit."

There is no birth connotation or message in baptism or his death on the cross, but there is the reality of the presence of water in the event of natural birth and ties in very well with Jesus's statement, "I tell you the truth, no one can see the kingdom of God unless he is born again." It could be entirely feasible that Jesus was talking of one event in the gospel of John, and John was talking about baptism as the testimony of Jesus's deity in 1 John 5:6. Further discussion is made available here as presentations by great scholars are considered.

John MacArthur agrees with those who accept baptism as the event referenced and makes this statement: "Some connect the phrase water and blood with Jesus' death when one of the soldiers pierced his side with a spear and immediately blood and water came out (John 19:34), but there is no reason to assume John had that incident in mind. It is also difficult to see how the piercing of Jesus's side was a divine witness to his deity; that was not a divine statement of anything, but rather a very human affirmation that Jesus was dead."

It is best to see the water here as a reference to Christ's baptism and the blood as a reference to his death. "Those two notable events bracketed the Lord's earthly ministry, and in both of them the Father testified concerning the Son." (260)

MacArthur says in another place concerning the reference to Jesus baptism in 1 John 5:6: "He (Jesus) was without sin (2 Corinthians 5:21; Hebrews 4:15; 7:26; 1 Peter 2:22 cf. John 8:46). It was still necessary for Jesus to be baptized. By doing so, he publicly identified with sinners." (261)

John's baptism was an indication of repentance. Mark 1:4 tells us, "And so John came baptizing in the desert region preaching a baptism of repentance." John MacArthur makes this statement concerning those baptized by John, "Their baptism was a public affirmation of repentance from sin, an external act symbolizing an internal reality." (262)

Those who are baptized today have a similar purpose with a different reality. Jesus has already forgiven the individual when confession is made for salvation. Therefore, baptism then becomes an outward manifestation of an inward rebirth which is the reality for a person who has already been saved.

It could be pointed out here as a reminder: As Jesus identified with sinners to fulfill all righteousness; Paul makes baptism a symbol of identification for the saved person in the symbolic burial and resurrection into Christ Jesus (Romans 6:3).

It is, however, a different context and a different message. Paul says: "Therefore, we should walk in the newness of life."

Please do not construe this to mean baptism is a part of salvation but that it is, in fact, an outer manifestation of an inner rebirth in Christ Jesus. Conversion is an event that occurs between an individual and God, baptism is an outward testimony that salvation has occurred.

The testimony of the blood is evidence accepted as proof of the reality of Christ. Requirement for a blood sacrifice was from the beginning. It has been the price for redemption and forgiveness of sin in the Scriptures since the beginning. When Adam and Eve sinned in the Garden of Eden, God killed an animal to provide a cover for their sin. Genesis 3:21, "The Lord made garments of skin for Adam and his wife and clothed them."

Guy H. King gives the reason for acceptance of Abel's gift over Cain's because requirement for blood sacrifice is required for forgiveness of sin.

The offering from Abel was one of blood. "There are some who preach, 'a bloodless gospel.'" That omission was the reason Cain's offering was not acceptable—it has no blood in it.

"All which was a figure of things to come." Hebrews 9:22 emphasizes the importance of the blood sacrifice and says, "In fact, the law requires that nearly everything be cleansed with blood, and without the shedding of blood there is no forgiveness of sin." (263)

Old Testament sacrifices were inadequate. The book of Leviticus is replete with what offerings are for what sins, and how the ceremony should proceed. In Leviticus, Aaron and his family were designated for the offering of sacrifices for certain sins and for certain times when the Hebrews would come together for cleansing of the whole nation. These offerings are referred to in Hebrews and contains an acknowledgement of the inadequacy of the sacrifice ceremony by Aaron and other high priests of his era.

In Hebrews 5:1–3 we are provided with the following information. "Every high priest is selected from among men and is appointed to represent them in matters related to God, to offer gifts and sacrifices for sins. He is able to deal gently with those who are ignorant and going astray, since he himself is subject to weakness. That is why he has to offer sacrifices for his own sins as well as for the sins of the people." Hebrews 9:7, "But only the high priest entered the inner room and that only once a year, never without blood which he offered for himself and for sins of the people." (264)

The adequacy of Jesus's blood must be a consideration because there was a certain group who believed the Holy Spirit set upon Christ at his baptism and departed before his crucifixion. It was important for John to emphasize that Jesus had not only come by water but also by blood. He makes that position very clear in the next line of 1cJohn 5:6, "He did not come by water only, but by water and blood."

The *Beacon Bible Commentary*, and many commentaries, inform us: "A Gnostic heresy of John's time held that Jesus was only a man, upon whom the Christ descended at baptism and from whom the Christ departed before the cross."(265)

There are many scriptures available to refute the assertion of the Gnostics. The position that Jesus was only a common man at the time of his crucifixion can easily be proven false by the events of that day. Matthew 27:45 reports a period of darkness of three hours during the day, "From the sixth hour to the ninth hour darkness came over all the land. About the ninth hour Jesus cried out in a loud voice, '*Eloi Eloi, lama sabachtni?*' which means, "My God, My God, why have you forsaken me?"

Although there are some who claim God never left Jesus's side during this time, it appears that the Bible presents a different story.

The tearing of the curtain in the temple is another mark of Jesus's divinity. It was torn from top to bottom. Pointing out that it was torn from top to bottom is important since it was beyond the reach of a man of ordinary height and it was much too heavy to be torn by hand.

At that moment, the curtain was torn in two from top to bottom, the earth shook and the rocks split, the tombs broke open and the bodies of many holy people who had died were raised to life. They came out of the tombs, and after Jesus's resurrection they went into the holy city and appeared too many people. (266)

That doesn't sound very ordinary to me. Add to that the resurrection story found in all the gospels and many other New Testament writings then it is very clear that he was who he said he was.

The reason that is so important is because if he were only a man, his death was in vain, and we are still in our sins. The apostle Paul emphatically denies that in 2 Corinthians 5:21 when he said, "God made him who knew no sin to be sin for us, so that in him we might become the righteousness of God."

There is a sin debt that must be paid. Romans 6:23 states very clearly: "The wages of sin is death, but the gift of God is eternal life through Jesus Christ his Son." By God's grace, through his Son it has been paid once for all: "He did not enter by means of the blood of goats and calves; but he entered the Most Holy Place once for all by his own blood, having obtained eternal redemption" (Hebrews 9:12).

The testimony of the Holy Spirit is considered as a testimony.

His personality qualifies him as a witness. Although it is implied by definition of the Greek word for *spirit*, (*pneuma*) that the Holy Spirit is breath or air. There is strong evidence that he is much more than that.

Donald Guthrie Points out in his book, *New Testament Theology*, that among many other evidences of his presence is that, "The Holy Spirit is a cleansing, purifying power and this certainly illuminates some of the Holy Spirit's work which come to clearer expression in the new testament." On page 531, he makes this revealing statement, "One other feature is the personal character of the spirit. This comes out clearly in the variety of functions the Holy Spirit performs, many of which would be unintelligible if not regarded as personal. In addition to this, the fact that Jesus spoke of another Paraclete shows that the Paraclete must be as personal as Jesus himself.

"These considerations completely override the neuter gender of the noun (*pneuma*) in Greek. Moreover, they are in full agreement with the striking use of the masculine pronoun (*ekeinos*) which underlines the personal characteristic of the Spirit. By no stretch of imagination can the teaching in these Paraclete sayings be made to refer to an impersonal force." (267)

The attribute that comes to the forefront in John's discussion concerning validation of Jesus Christ is found in 1 John 5:6c when he points out: "And it is the Spirit who testifies because the Spirit is truth."

History qualifies him to be a witness. He was there at the creation of the world; the Bible gives him an active part in the creation: "Now the earth was formless and empty, darkness was over the face of the deep, and the Spirit of God was hovering over the waters" (Genesis 1:2).

He was there at the conception. Luke 1:35 records a conversation between Mary and an angel concerning his part in it. "The angel of the Lord answered, 'The Holy Spirit will come upon you, and the power of the most high will overshadow you, so the holy one to be born will be called, the Son of God.'"

He was there at the baptism. Matthew 3:16 proclaims his presence: "As soon as Jesus was baptized he went up out of the water. At that moment heaven opened and he saw the Spirit of God descending like a dove and lighting on him."

Although the Bible doesn't say specifically that the Holy Spirit was at either of the following events, the events certainly imply his presence. He was there at the crucifixion; he was there at the resurrection; he was there at the ascension; his purpose qualifies him as a witness.

1. His primary purpose is to glorify Christ, Jesus informed the disciples of his coming and his purpose to bring glory to the name of Jesus: "He will bring glory to me by taking from what is mine and making it known to you" (John 16:14).

2. Jesus declared his purpose was to convince the world of sin, righteousness and salvation: "When he comes, he will convict the world of guilt in regard to sin, and righteousness, and judgment" (John 16:8).

3. Jesus stated that his purpose was to enable believers: "When the Counselor comes, whom I will send unto you from my Father, the Spirit of truth who goes out from the Father, he will testify about me" (John 15:26).

   a. He enables us in understanding: "I have much more to say to you, more than you can bear. But when he, the Spirit of truth comes, he will guide you into all truth" (John 16:12–13).

   b. He enables us through the gift of assurance: "And this is how we know he lives in us: we know it by the Spirit he gave us" (1 John 3:23).

   c. He enables us by empowerment: "But you will receive power when the Holy Spirit comes on you" (Acts 1:8).

4. His purpose was to validate the testimony of the water and the blood: "For there are three that testify: The Spirit, the water and the blood; and the three are in agreement" (1 John 5:7).

5. His purpose is to draw those who would be saved to Christ. Guy H. King informs us, "This is the beginning of the explanation of every conversion or regeneration. The initiative is always with him." (268)

His representation qualifies the Holy Spirit as a witness. John points out: "We accept man's testimony, but God's testimony is greater because it is the testimony of God, which he has given about his Son" (John 5:9).

There is a testimony within us that serves as a witness.

John produces yet another way we can know we are saved when he informs us: "Anyone who believes in the Son of God has this testimony in his heart" (1 John 5:10).

Here is the dividing line between the haves and the have nots, once again, so let us discuss what is meant by this witness within.

There is to be considered internalizing or digesting the change that has taken place in one's life. There is a change of mind, a change of heart, and a change of behavior.

When an individual changes his or her mind about God, many changes happen. Believing creates a desire for fellowship and learning.

Believing creates a desire to be like Jesus. That doesn't always happen instantly; it takes time to discard old habits and learn new things but there is that testimony in our heart.

That kind of believing will only come to one who has had a change of heart. The adage, "Where the heart goes, the heels will soon follow," is still as true as it has ever been.

If there has been no change of mind, heart, or behavior, John says, "Anyone who does not believe God has made him out to be a liar." Joining a church won't save you. Cleaning up your life won't save you. It must come from the heart. Do you have a testimony of faith and salvation in your heart?

Pastor Keith Miller has made the point in his sermon that changing the shape or looks of our body has nothing to do with changing our heart. That's true with me. How about you? 1 John 5:11–12 sums it up this way in verse, "God has given us eternal life, and this life is in his Son. He who has the Son has life. He who does not have the Son does not have life." Only God and you know. Do you have a testimony within?

CHAPTER 24

Light on the Path of Righteousness Reveals the Conclusion of the Search

1 John 5:12–16

Here, once again, is a reminder that John is not writing to the lost world but to a church made up of Christians who are questioning their salvation because a certain faction, or group, has come into their midst and taught heresy as new truth and caused confusion among them: "I write these things to you who believe in the name of the Son of God so that you may know that you have eternal life" (1 John 5:13).

The question of salvation must be settled. John makes the difference in being lost or saved very clear. He simply states, "He who has the Son has life; He who does not have the Son of God does not have life" (1 John 5:12).

That's a serious statement. That is a statement of life or death. But right now, you might not be sure it includes you. Perhaps you somehow have concluded that Christ is the Son of God and the Savior of the world but you don't qualify for the gift of eternal life.

J. Vernon McGee advises, "The question is, do you have Christ? Is he your Savior? Are you trusting him in such a way that no one on earth or in heaven can shake your confidence in him? My friend, if you haven't come to that point, you haven't come anywhere at all.

To be saved means you trust Christ, and it means you have Christ as your Savior." (270)

The decision is really yours to make. Allow me to paint a word picture of a possible conversation between an unsaved person and our Lord; maybe it will help your understanding and bring the assurance you are looking for.

Jesus's expression of love:

"Behold, I stand at the door and knock," said Jesus.
"But my life is a mess."
"Behold, I stand at the door and knock."
"But I am a liar, a thief, and cheat."
"Behold, I stand at the door and knock."
"But I'm a hypocrite."
"Behold, I stand at the door and knock."
"But I'm not good enough."
"Behold, I stand at the door and Knock."
"But I have always been rejected."
"Behold, I stand at the door and knock."

"Here I Am! I stand at the door and knock. If anyone opens the door, I will come in and eat with him and he with me."
"But Lord, I have to clean up a place for you to sit."
"I will clean it up, just let me in!"
"But Lord I have nothing to offer you." (Revelation 3:20)

"I have something for you. I have come that they may have life, and have it to the full." (John 10:10b)

"What do I have to do, Lord? I'm so confused and uncertain. There is so much I don't know!"

"That if you confess with your mouth, Jesus is Lord, and believe in your heart that God raised him from the dead, you will be saved." (Romans 10:9)

"But, I can't be saved—no emotional cataclysmic event has occurred in my life."
"Believe in the Lord Jesus Christ and you will be saved." (Acts 16:31)

"But maybe I'm not one of the chosen."
"He is patient with you, not wanting anyone to perish, but everyone to come to repentance." (1 Peter 3:9)

"But what about John 6:44 where Jesus said, 'No one can come to me unless the Father who sent me draws him.'"
"The fact that we are having this conversation is evidence that you have been drawn by the Father to respond to your call to salvation."
"But there must be something for me to do!"
"There is. 'Everyone who calls on the name of the Lord will be saved' (Acts 2:21). *Open the door!*"
"If anyone hears and opens the door, I will come in and eat with him and he with me." (Revelation 3:20)

When the reality of Christ is realized, it is evidence of a conclusion.

From the beginning of this writing, John has attempted to offer Christ as the reality. He revealed him as the light of the world. He revealed him as God's love personified in a sinful world, and now he reveals him as the eternal life. The last verses of 1 John are a sort of summary of all that.

Verse twelve is the conclusion of assurance. It seems to me John is sort of saying, "Now we have looked at the evidence." Now it comes down to this conclusion: "He who has the Son of God has life, he who does not have the Son of God does not have life" (1 John 5:12).

Guy H. King claims, "John and Paul are full of sublime certitudes because they base their certainty, not on their own merit, or power, but only on the wondrous mercy and grace of the almighty God." (271)

1 John 5:13 offers the assurance so desperately searched for by so many and the purpose for writing this letter: "I write these things to you who believe in the name of the Son of God so that you may know that you have eternal life."

The search for assurance has been completed on paper. Now it is up to the searcher to prayerfully search his or her own heart and come to realize that God is for him and grace is available to her and that salvation is real and available to anyone who seeks after it.

Knowing one has eternal life brings internal change. One of the changes that come about is the joy of knowing we have eternal life.

It was raining that day. One of those almost rains that come in the South. I was having trouble with a deacon. He wanted me to report to him more often—I guess. When I am troubled, I walk.

That day I went for a long walk. During the walk, I came to a small bridge on a country road; I sat on the edge of the bridge with my feet dangling over the edge in agony of thought and deep prayer for a long time. Finally, I walked back home to find my baby daughter sitting in the middle of my bed with a new tape recorder I had just bought singing, "Because he lives, I can face tomorrow." She's gone now, killed by a drunk driver several years ago, but the memory and the lesson lingers on. Because he lives, I can face tomorrow. Because there is eternal life and because one day we can celebrate together.

Although some translations and commentators look at this verse differently, many cling to 1 Corinthians 13:12 KJV as a promise of knowing loved ones when we get to heaven and learning all the things we cannot know now. Paul offers this hope this way to the church at Corinth: "For now we see through a glass, darkly; but then face to face; now I know in part; but then shall I know even as I am also known."

The apostle Paul brought this hope to life: "If only for this life we have hope in Christ, we are to be pitied more than all men, but Christ has indeed been raised from the dead, the first-fruits of those who have fallen asleep"

He continues to offer that hope by quoting an Old Testament Scripture in 1 Corinthians 15:55–56: "Where, O death is your victory? Where, O death is your sting? The sting of death is sin, and the power of sin is the law. But thanks be to God! He gives us the victory through our Lord Jesus Christ."

There is joy in the expectancy of full realization. John MacArthur describes his perception of day and states, "On that glorious day, they will experience their adoption as sons, the redemption of [the] body (Romans 8:23; cf. Philippians 3:21; 1 John 3:2). Then the glory of eternal life—the power of the trinity that works within them (cf. Ephesians 3:16–19)—will shine through them unclouded by their mortal bodies." (156) (272)

Reflection brings to memory many hymns over the years that express the expectancy of a glorious future life. The apostle Paul points to that hope this way, "I consider that our present sufferings are not worth comparing with the glory that will be revealed in us. The creation waits in eager expectation for the sons of God to be revealed. For the creation was subjected to frustration, not by its' own choice, but by the will of the one who subjected it, in hope that the creation itself will be liberated from the bondage of decay, and brought into the glorious freedom of the children of God." (273)

There is the boldness of promise. So many promises are made then not kept by those around us. I started two other books some years ago, in cooperation with a fellow church member who was well qualified on the computer which I was not and am still not. She became angry with me about something I had nothing to do with and took those manuscripts and refused to return them. The fact that one of them was incomplete and the other one was of no use to her without my support was irrelevant to her. She broke her promise to me and wasted several hours of her time and mine. I could give you a long list of broken promises, but you probably have your own; I could be one of those on your list.

We have the blessed assurance in this life and the one to come that there is one who keeps all his promises—that is, our Lord and Savior, Jesus Christ. Galatians 3:14 offers an example of the certainty of God's promises, "He redeemed us in order that the blessing given to Abraham might come to the Gentiles through Christ Jesus, so that by faith we might receive the promise of the Spirit." In the following scriptures he elaborates, and in doing so, substantiates the validity of God's promises:

> Brothers, let me take an example from everyday life. Just as no one can set aside or add to a human covenant that has been duly established, so it is in this case. For if inheritance depends on the law, then it no longer depends on a promise; but God in his grace gave it to Abraham through a promise. (Galatians 3:15–18)
>
> Although there are those who would like to wait as long as possible in the hope of winning loved ones, or for other reasons, there are those who are anxious for his coming. To those Paul has this message: "The Lord is not slow in keeping his promise, as some understand slowness. He is patient with you, not wanting anyone to perish but everyone to come to repentance." (2 Peter 3:9)

Because it provides confidence it the intangible, or unseen reality, there is boldness in faith.

John offers this summary statement after considering all the ways we can know we are saved: "This is the confidence we have in approaching God" (1 John 5:14).

J. Vernon McGee inform us that, "This word confidence actually means boldness." (274) The boldness of our faith comes from believing the promise. Christians believe the promise because by faith, we believe Jesus Christ tore the curtain between man and God by becoming our advocate. The writer of Hebrews especially expresses this opportunity for boldness: "Let us therefore come boldly to the throne of grace that we might obtain mercy and find grace in time of need" (Hebrews 4:16 KJV).

1 John 5:14b, "That if we ask anything according to his will he hears us."

Guy H. King makes his position on the importance of faith clear: "Faith is the principle of Christian life—not only at its beginning, but in its continuing all the way through." (275)

Baker's Dictionary of Theology identifies faith as both a noun and a verb and offers this description, "Unqualified acceptance of and exclusive dependence on, the meditation of the Son as alone securing the mercy of the Father." He also says, "The nature of faith, according to the NT, is to live by the truth it receives: faith resting on God's promise, gives thanks for God's grace by working for God's glory." (276)

This description of the nature of faith by *Baker's Dictionary of Theology* reflects the words found in James 2:23, "And the scripture was fulfilled that says, 'Abraham believed God, and it was credited to him as righteousness.'"

That sounds as if all you need to do to be righteous is believe, and it is; but the faith James is talking about is more than a casual realization. He makes it very clear in the previous verse that the kind of faith that makes one righteous is the kind that motivates to action. There James has pointed out that the works (Lifestyle) of Abraham and his faith became one to bring about righteousness: "You see that his faith and his actions were working together, and his faith was made complete by what he did" (James 2:22). It is true that works is not a part of the plan of salvation, insofar as your being saved is concerned, but the Bible clearly teaches that works is a fruit of faith.

The condition stated in the model prayer; Matthew 6:10, "Your kingdom come, your will be done on earth as it is in heaven." Was just as relevant in John's day, several years later. And it is still relevant today. 1 John 5:14, "According to his will," makes an important statement. The believer should be in tune with God to the extent that selfishness and greed are not a part of prayer life.

This might be a good time to remember the prayer of Jesus in the garden of Gethsemane: "Yet not as I will, but as you will" (Matthew 26:39b). If one is earnestly seeking the will of God and his glory, prayer will follow that pattern. That's how we can know our prayers are answered. 1 John 5:15 tells us, "And if we know that he hears us—whatever we ask—we know we have what we ask of him." That must be dependent on what we ask for governed by a relationship with God that enables us to discern his will to some extent.

John MacArthur says," The sure promise of God is that when believers boldly and freely come to him with their requests, he will hear and answer. "If we ask anything according to his will." John wrote, "He hears us." And we know that he hears us in whatever we ask, we know that we have the requests which we have asked from him". Hearing in this context refers to more than merely God's being aware of believers' requests; it also means that he grants "the requests which we have asked from him." That is nothing less than a blank check to ask God for anything, but it comes with one important qualifier: the requests must be "according to his will." (277)

Donald Guthrie points out that: "The place and importance of prayers in the communities must be noticed. Paul himself includes many prayers in his epistles and this in itself shows the importance he attached to prayer for his converts." (278)

There is the condition of discernment concerning what one should pray for.

1 John 5:16, "If anyone sees his brother commit a sin that does not lead to death, he should pray and God will give him life."

John MacArthur says, "Evidently John and his readers knew what the 'sin leading to death' was, since no explanation has been given, but its exact meaning is difficult for us to determine." (279)

Speculation concerning "the unpardonable sin" ranges from rejection of the Holy Spirit to saying certain words that "take God's name in vain." J. Vernon McGee reminds us of some who apparently committed the "sin unto death." Moses was condemned to die before the children of Israel entered the Promised Land. He was, however, allowed to look over into it. Ananias and Saphira were instantly put to death because of their deceit and lies. (280) There are possibly

Christians who are taken home today because of their shameful behavior, but we are not qualified to say who they are or even if that's the reason.

The truth is, we just don't know what the unforgiveable sin is, and speculation only accomplishes more confusion.

We should pray fervently and often for every need and person that comes in need of prayer; after all, it is God who must make the call as to right or relevance. Romans 8:33 seems applicable here: "Who will bring any charge against those whom God has chosen? It is God who justifies."

Paul tells the church at Thessalonica: "Be joyful always; pray continually; give thanks in all circumstances, for this is God's will for you in Christ Jesus" (1 Thessalonians 5:16).

There is the promise of answered prayer in several scriptures. Following is a quote from Pastor Hybels, as copied from *Nelson's Complete Book of Stories*:

> If the request is wrong, God says no.
> If the timing is wrong, God says slow.
> If you are wrong, God says grow.
> But if the request is right, the timing is right, and
> you are right, God says go. (281)

CHAPTER 25

Light on the Path of Righteousness Reveals the Indwelling Christ as a Deterrent from Sin

1 John 5:18–21

Jamieson, Fausset Brown Commentary explains 1 John 5:18 in such a way that it corresponds with the rest of the New Testament teachings and specifically with the statement made in 1 John 3:9. "No one who is born of God will continue to sin because God's seed remains in him; he cannot go on sinning because he has been born of God."

Although it might seem tedious, it makes a very clear statement. Their explanation for the phrase "keepeth himself" in KJV and 1 John 5:18 is stated thus: "Anyone born of God does not continue to sin; the one who was born of God keeps him safe, and the evil one cannot harm him.

"The Vulgate translates, 'The having been begotten of God keepeth *him*.' So one of the oldest manuscripts reads, 'so *alford*.' Literally, 'He having been begotten of God (nominative pendent) it (the divine generation implied in the nominative) keepeth him.'"

So 1 John 3:9, "His seed remaineth in him." Still, in English Version reading, God's working by his spirit inwardly, and man's working under the power of that spirit as a responsible agent is what often occurs elsewhere. That God must keep us, if we are to keep ourselves from evil is certain.

The phrase "we know" is a very important way to begin this summary of previous lessons and events. This letter addresses the topic of knowing, then lays out several truths and observations to establish the fact that we know. How do we know? We know we have eternal salvation when His spirit communicates with our spirit. We know we have eternal life because we love others. We know we have eternal life because we do not practice sinning, etc. The knowing is important because it is in knowing that we are able to resist evil.

Jamieson, Fausset, and Brown enforces the truth that it is not by our strength only that we remain free from sin but by the power and grace of God. (283) We are free from slavery to sin because we have an anointing. John informs his readers emphatically: "But you have an anointing from the Holy One, and all of you know the truth" (1 John 2:20).

Real Christians are free from the power of sin because we know who we are. We are free from the slavery of sin because our Lord lives in us; Christians do not continually sin because we know we are children of God. 1 John 5:19 clearly states, "We know we are children of God." That knowing we are children in the family of God is significant in that it not only affects our future, it determines our attitude and behavior. When the apostle Paul informed us in 2 Corinthians 5:17: "Therefore if anyone is in Christ, he is a new creation; the old has gone, the new has come!" He brought us back to Jesus's statement in John 3:3, "I tell you the truth, no one can see the kingdom of God unless he is born again."

There has been a change of disposition in the individual who becomes a Christian. From the first man, Adam, there is an inherited genetic disposition to sin. In Jesus Christ, there is a spiritual disposition to righteousness. 1 John 4:4, "You, dear children, are from God and have overcome them because greater is he that is in you than the one who is in the world."

We keep ourselves from the practice of sin because children of God have a deposit that guarantees a home in glory. The apostle Paul informs the church in Ephesus and us: "And you also were included in Christ when you heard the word of truth, the gospel (good news) of your salvation. Having believed, you were marked in him with a seal, the promised Holy Spirit, who is a deposit guaranteeing our inheritance until redemption of those who are God's possession—to the praise of his glory." (284)

Looking forward to that day with great hopes motivates every true Christian because he or she knows about the promise in Colossians 1:26–27.

"The mystery that has been hidden for ages and generations, but now is disclosed to the saints. To them God has chosen to make known among the Gentiles the glorious riches of his mystery, which is Christ in you, the hope of glory." (285)

Real Christians do not practice sin because they believe and acknowledge that Jesus came in the flesh.

First John 5:20, "We know also that the Son of God has come and given us understanding."

History across races and nations verifies that Jesus came and walked among the people during his time on earth. The apostle Paul and others have offered irrefutable evidence of the death, burial and resurrection of our Lord. 1 Corinthians 15:3–8 lists the minimum number of witnesses to his appearance after his resurrection as more than five hundred. It seems appropriate to agree with a certain program on television titled *I Don't Have Enough Faith to Be an Atheist* because, after all the evidence for his life death and resurrection, it would take a strong belief to overcome the evidence offered, not only in scripture but also by several other sources.

The record of the first coming of Christ is important because it is the foundation for the second. It is also important for the foundation of everything Christians believe and experience of the promises extended to us when he was here. Christians who accept the validity of his having come before, understand his promises to us and the revelation of certain truths provided to Christians through the anointing of Jesus Christ.

Idol worship was and is prevalent. There were many idols at the time of John's writing. There were many idols in Abraham's day and Moses's day. There have always been idols. In the book of Exodus, those who lived in that period of time had a golden calf. Today that golden calf takes on many shapes, colors, and configurations, but the same purpose exists.

The desire for something concrete to hang on to or look at is emotionally satisfying. Remember what the Israelites told Aaron? Exodus 32:1, "Make us Gods that will go before us." Apparently, they had forgotten the cloud by day and the fire by night that had guided them previously. They wanted a tangible god they could see and touch. Idol worshippers want the same thing today. It could be a new pickup truck, or a new boat, or a football game, or a baseball game, or some other kind of game, or even fishing, or many other things considered more important than God.

A definition for idol used by a myriad of pastors, preachers, and teachers throughout the Christian world is anything one elevates in his or her life as more important than God.

One commentator said, "There were many idols in John's day. There are more today." Ultimately, the sin is not in the object, but in the act of making it more important than God. Is anything in your life more important to you than God? Then let me remind you of this admonition—keep yourself from idols!

ENDNOTES

1. *The Preacher's Homiletic Commentary* on 1 John, etc., Baker Book House, Grand Rapids Michigan, page 232.
2. Acts 16:30–33, Kenneth Barker, general editor, New International Version Bible, Grand Rapids Michigan, Copyright: 1973, 1978, 1984 by International Bible Society
3. Acts 16:31, NIV.
4. Guy H. King, *The Fellowship*, Marshall, Morgan & Scott, Ltd., 116 Baker Street, London, WIM 2BB, page 14.
5. John 14:2
6. A personal story of a miracle in Germany.
7. Philippians 2:9, NIV.
8. *Unger's Bible Dictionary*, The Moody Bible Institute of Chicago, page 665.
9. Crucifixion confirmed by historians and geologists.
10. Matthew 27:50, NIV.
11. Thallus on the darkness at noon (e.wickipedia.org/wiki/crucifixion/darkness).
12. Jennifer Viegas, Discovery News, as reported on *International Review*, NBC News.
13. 1 Corinthians 15:4, NIV.
14. Chester E. Schuler, a boy flying a kite.
15. 1 Thessalonians 4:16–17
16. *New World Dictionary*
17. Ibid.
18. *Baker's Dictionary of Theology*
19. John MacArthur

20. Returning from a night mission in Vietnam as an example of God's light.
21. Hebrews 10:25
22. Ephesians 3:31
23. *Easton's Illustrated Bible Dictionary*
24. *Webster's New World Dictionary*
25. *The Holman Illustrated Bible Dictionary*: Holman Bible Publishers, Nashville Tennessee
26. Genesis 3:8–9, NIV.
27. Exodus 3:3, NIV.
28. Quote from a previous Southern Baptist Convention president.
29. A time of terror and a revelation of my father's faith.
30. A field exercise where I was surrounded by army tanks.
31. *The Holman Illustrated Bible Dictionary*
32. Ibid.
33. *The World Book Encyclopedia*
34. 1 John 1:6, NIV.
35. *The New Commentary on the Whole Bible*
36. *Adam Clarke's Commentary*
37. Donald Guthrie, *New Testament Theology*
38. Guy H. King
39. A little boy who refused to sit in his seat.
40. J. Vernon McGee
41. A young Christian who aspired to leadership who lived an unchristian lifestyle.
42. Matthew 5:13, NIV.
43. Matthew 24:37, NKJV.
44. *Adam Clarke's Commentary*
45. Harold T. Bryson
46. *The World Book Encyclopedia*
47. A personal experience where I almost lost my life because of a loose nut.
48. A young lady refused to make a profession of faith because she "had a few more wild oats to sow."
49. Matthew 28:19–20, NIV.
50. Baptized with whisky coke while stationed in Korea.

51. An older man saved in Kansas.
52. Witnessing to a soldier named Doss.
53. Adam Clarke
54. Ibid.
55. *The Matthew Henry Commentary*
56. Numbers 31:7, NIV.
57. Matthew 25:24–25, NJKV.
58. A young lady who stopped attending church because she didn't want to change her lifestyle.
59. Genesis 3:6, NIV.
60. Luke 12:18, NIV.
61. Harold C. Gardener, *The Treasury of Religious Spiritual Quotations.*
62. Donald Guthrie, *New Testament Theology: Thematic Study.*
63. Author unknown.
64. Donald Guthrie, *New Testament Theology.*
65. *Baker's Dictionary of Theology*
66. Donald Guthrie
67. *Baker's Theological Dictionary*
68. J. Vernon McGee
69. Jerry Stafford, *Emotions: Controlled or Controlling.*
70. Training pigeons to perform certain behaviors.
71. *Baker's Dictionary of Theology*
72. The story of a maple tree that was rotten inside.
73. Herbert W. Byrne, *Reclaiming Inactive Church Members.*
74. Baptism of a man who was living in adultery.
75. J. Vernon McGee
76. Revelation 21:8, NIV.
77. *The Preachers Homiletic Commentary*
78. Ibid.
79. *The Holman Bible Handbook*
80. Genesis 3:23–24, NIV.
81. *The Matthew Henry Commentary*
82. Alexander the Great as an example.
83. *Matthew Henry Commentary*
84. *The Beacon Bible Commentary*

85. *Adam Clarke's Commentary*
86. *The Preacher's Homiletic Commentary*
87. *The Preacher's Homiletic Commentary*
88. Genesis 3:17, NIV.
89. Romans 5:14, NKJV.
90. A pastor who preached a sermon he believed he had been called to preach.
91. 1 Samuel 3:2–10, NIV.
92. A young preacher who saw two letters in the clouds and thought it was a call to preach.
93. J. Vernon McGee
94. Romans 2:14–15, NIV.
95. John MacArthur
96. J. Vernon McGee
97. Revelation 20:12–15.
98. 2 Thessalonians 1:8
99. 2 Peter 1:3–4
100. Dr. Joe Dubose, past president of Graceville Baptist Bible Institute, Graceville, Florida, from 1977–1999.
101. 2 Samuel 12:4–7, NIV.
102. Wally Metz
103. Luke 24:13–32
104. Donald Guthrie, *New Testament Theology*
105. Ibid.
106. J. Vernon McGee
107. The murder of two babies in Wichita Kansas.
108. Revelation 20:12–15, NIV.
109. *The New Commentary on the Whole Bible*
110. Donald Guthrie, *New Testament Theology*
111. Guy H. King, *The Fellowship*
112. A little boy who refused to sit.
113. A young man who aspired to leadership in a church but behaved in an un-Christian way.
114. Matthew 5:13, NIV.
115. *The International Standard Bible Encyclopedia*
116. Ibid.

117. A personal example of obedience.
118. *Baker's Dictionary of Theology*
119. Ibid.
120. An example of a lack of grace.
121. Guy H. King
122. J. Vernon McGee
123. *The Holman Illustrated Bible Dictionary*
124. 1 John 2:16, NKJV.
125. Harold T. Bryson
126. 1 Peter 5:2–3, NIV.
127. Guy H. King
128. Ibid.
129. Matthew Henry
130. A time of terror that emphasizes how temporary material things are.
131. 1 Peter 1:3, NIV.
132. Romans 8:37–39, NIV.
133. *The Holman Illustrated Dictionary*
134. An example of excessive self-pride.
135. J. Vernon McGee
136. *The Preacher's Homiletic Commentary*
137. Matthew 13:3–8, NIV.
138. Psalms 1:1–3, NKJV.
139. J. Vernon McGee
140. Matthew 10:37, NKJV.
141. J. Vernon McGee
142. Ibid.
143. *The Preacher's Homiletic Commentary*
144. *Holman Illustrated Bible Dictionary*
145. Acts 10:37, NIV.
146. Richard Stephens, pastor of Grace Mennonite Church.
147. William Barclay
148. Ibid.
149. Exodus 20:3, NIV.
150. A young Korean Girl singing "Yes, Jesus Loves Me."

151. River Road Baptist Chapel, Hopewell, Virginia, approximately 1971–1972.
152. Guy H. King
153. Revelation 20:4, NIV.
154. J. Vernon McGee
155. Matthew 25:29, NIV.
156. Footnote in NIV pertaining to Matthew 25:29
157. J. Vernon McGee
158. An incident in Virginia where a little boy was playing in a snake den.
159. *Baker's Dictionary of Theology*
160. Guy H. King
161. *Baker's Dictionary of Theology*
162. Romans 7:7–12, NIV.
163. *Baker's Dictionary of Theology*
164. Guy H. King
165. Colossians 2:13–14, NKJV.
166. Romans 6:15–18, NIV.
167. Free
168. Preparing horses to sell to the army.
169. 900 women, men, and children led to suicide and murder by Jim Jones on a little island named by him as Jonesboro.
170. *The Holman Illustrated Bible Dictionary*
171. Romans 6:3–4, NIV.
172. Romans 10:1–4
173. John MacArthur
174. Zechariah 3:3, NKJV.
175. Matthew Henry
176. Ibid.
177. John MacArthur
178. Revelation 21:8, NIV.
179. John MacArthur
180. Ibid.
181. A personal test of faith.
182. Guy H. King
183. Harold T. Bryson

184. J. Vernon McGee
185. A church member who set an example of Christian conduct.
186. Walter B. Night, *Knights Master Book of New Illustrations*, "Can you feel the tug?" by Chester E. Fuller, Grand Rapids, Michigan; W. M. Eerdmans Publishing Company, page 43.
187. Guy H. King
188. 2 Corinthians 3:6, NKJV.
189. John MacArthur
190. Matthew Henry
191. 2 Corinthians 5:17, NIV.
192. Galatians 5:22, NIV.
193. John MacArthur
194. Childhood medicine administered by mama.
195. Donald Guthrie, *New Testament Theology*
196. NIV marginal notes 1 John 4:1–2, speak of Gnostic Doctrine
197. Barnes Notes
198. *Baker's Dictionary of Theology*
199. Philippians 2:6–8, NIV.
200. 1 John 4:2–3
201. *Unger's Bible Dictionary*
202. Donald Guthrie, *New Testament Theology*
203. 1 Thessalonians 4:16–17, NIV.
204. 1 Corinthians 13:1–3
205. Romans 4:11
206. Elton Trueblood
207. Ilion T. Jones, a Southern Baptist Extension study course
208. Barnes Notes CP, Quickverse 2010
209. Matthew 23:23
210. Gail McGrew, *Reader's Digest*, The Treasury of Religious Quotations
211. 1 Corinthians 13:4–7, NIV.
212. J. Vernon McGee
213. John MacArthur
214. A sermon by Dr. W. A. Criswell several years ago.
215. 2 Corinthians 11:23–26, NIV.
216. Harold T. Bryson

217. *The World Book Encyclopedia*
218. Guy H. King
219. J. Vernon McGee
220. Hebrews 10:1–7, NIV.
221. *World Book Encyclopedia*
222. Harold T. Bryson
223. Ibid.
224. J. Vernon McGee
225. Guy H. King
226. 2 Corinthians 5:16–19, NIV.
227. Guy H. King
228. Ibid.
229. 1 Corinthians 6:19–20, NIV.
230. Barnes Notes
231. Ibid.
232. Ibid.
233. *The Holman Bible Dictionary*
234. Philippians 2:1–4, NIV.
235. 1 Corinthians 13:1–3, NIV.
236. Barnes Notes
237. Guy H. King
238. *The Holman Illustrated Bible Dictionary*
239. Guy H. King
240. Harold T. Bryson
241. Joshua 5:14, NIV.
242. John MacArthur
243. *The New Commentary*
244. Ephesians 1:13–14, NIV.
245. *Adam Clarke's Commentary*
246. 1 Peter 1:3, NIV.
247. Numbers 13:6, NIV.
248. Judges 7:19, NIV.
249. Confession of lack of faith as a fifteen-year-old boy.
250. Harold T. Bryson
251. John Hick, *The Myth of God Incarnate*, published by SCM Press, 1977.

252. Harold T. Bryson
253. Ibid.
254. *Josephus*. A series of books relating Jewish history from the perspective of Josephus (sacred -texts.com/jud/josephus/).
255. Matthew 3:13–17, NIV.
256. Matthew Henry
257. *Beacon Bible Commentary*
258. John MacArthur
259. Ibid.
260. John MacArthur
261. Guy H. King
262. Hebrews 5:1–3, NIV.
263. *The Beacon Bible Commentary*
264. Matthew 27:51, NIV>
265. Donald Guthrie, *New Testament Theology*
266. Guy H. King
267. Pastor Keith Miller, then pastor of First Baptist Enid, Oklahoma, now missionary to China.
268. J. Vernon McGee
269. Guy H. King
270. John MacArthur
271. Romans 8:18–21, NIV.
272. J. Vernon McGee
273. Guy H. King
274. *Baker's Dictionary of Theology*
275. John MacArthur
276. Donald Guthrie
277. John MacArthur
278. J. Vernon McGee
279. Pastor Hybels, *Nelson's Complete Book of Stories*
280. *Jamieson, Fawcett, Brown Commentary*
281. Ibid.
282. Ephesians 1:13–14, NIV.
283. Ephesians 1:26–27, NIV.

ABOUT THE AUTHOR

J erry Stafford is a former pastor and church planter who has retired from the army. His ministry has extended over a period of fifty years in several states and abroad. He holds a Bachelor of Arts degree in psychology, a master of behavioral science degree, master of ministries degree, and doctor of ministries degree.

This is his fourth published book. The other three are: *Searching for Certainty, The Saints of Bogby Baptist Church* and *The Greatest?*

CPSIA information can be obtained
at www.ICGtesting.com
Printed in the USA
FFOW03n0521200518
46704600-48805FF